CALIFORNIA COUNTRY STYLE

CALIFORNIA COUNTRY STYLE

DIANE DORRANS SAEKS

Photographs by David Duncan Livingston

CHRONICLE BOOKS

SAN FRANCISCO

Halcyon days

—Diane Dorrans Saeks

Library of Congress Cataloging-in-Publication Data available.

ISBN-10: 0-8118-5181-8
ISBN-13: 978-0-8118-5181-7

Manufactured in China

Designed by Madeleine Corson Design, San Francisco

Distributed in Canada by Raincoast Books
9050 Shaughnessy Street
Vancouver, British Columbia V6P 6E5

10 9 8 7 6 5 4 3 2 1

Chronicle Books LLC
85 Second Street
San Francisco, California 94105

www.chroniclebooks.com

Late Summer Landscape (page 1) The Rudd Vineyards and Winery
in the Napa Valley.

Languid Living (page 2) Healdsburg interior designer Myra Hoefer
creates a French country mood in her Ivy House living room. The
floor of practical sea-grass matting contrasts with the superb silk
curtains from the Silk Trading Company and gold-framed Wade
Hoefer prints and paintings.

Front Cover Interior designer Steven Volpe practices the art of classical
French style with modern flair. Louis would love it.

The chic decor speaks with a distinct French accent. The 5,500-
square-foot residence stands on a quiet tree-lined street in Hillsborough,
Northern California, surrounded by Le Notre–style box parterres and
citrus trees. It's filled with California sunshine and a collection of
museum-worthy California paintings.

"My ideal was a classic Parisian town house but modern and very
Californian," said Volpe, who opened Hedge Gallery in partnership
with Roth Martin to showcase their Hedge collection of French
forties–style furniture and French vintage furniture collections. "My
clients are Francophiles, and the Parisian style followed naturally from
their passion for French history and art. But we wanted it to feel at
home in Northern California, very fresh and relaxed."

Thanks to Steven Volpe's in-depth knowledge of French historic
styles and his passion for French forties decor balanced with his desire
to shake things up a bit, the elegant French manor is more fun king
than Sun King.

Pale parchment-colored faux-bois painted wall paneling, an abaca
matting carpet from the Waldo Collection in Los Angeles, and waxed
oak beams give the living room/media room a sense of calm. The
Italian sofa is upholstered in Swedish leather. A quartet of bronze
candlesticks are by Ted Muehling, New York. Chartreuse cashmere
throw by Hermes.

CONTENTS

ESCAPE TO THE COUNTRY

———

A GOLDEN MORNING IN CALIFORNIA BEGINS. ACROSS SUN-STRUCK VINEYARDS THE MISTS ARE EVAPORATING. A LIGHT BREEZE SHIMMERS OVER THE SURFACE OF A SWIMMING POOL. SUMMER SCENTS OF LAVENDER AND JASMINE AND CÉCILE BRUNNER roses swirl through the air. After a walk along hillside trails, it's time for breakfast on the dappled terrace, and later, a drive to the farmers' market. Bounty in the bulging string bags includes figs and earthy lettuces and golden tomatoes and juicy white peaches for lunch.

In Healdsburg, artist Wade Hoefer puts down his coffee cup and picks up his first paintbrush of the day. On canvas, he captures a timeless river curving through an oneiric landscape that could be in nearby Dry Creek Valley, Big Sur, or even eighteenth-century Napa Valley.

Enveloped in her green world of walnut groves and ancient oak trees, Ann Getty clips an armful of red and yellow zinnias and carries them into her country house, where they're arranged in antique Indian silver bowls.

It's perfect growing weather at The French Laundry garden in Yountville, and pale green stalks of cardoon are almost ready for the day's menu. Spinach and English peas sprout beneath the Napa Valley sun, gathering flavor from the terroir for chef Thomas Keller's inspiration. At The French Laundry, perfection is in the details.

At Manka's in Inverness, chef/owner Margaret Gradé leaves the kitchen door unlocked so that organic farmers from nearby Bolinas and Point Reyes Station can bring in their peas and beans, amber-hued honey, and the sweetest strawberries. Cheesemaker Soyoung Scanlan arrives with a tray of delicate Metronome, Nocturne, and Adagio cheeses made at her Andante Dairy in Santa Rosa. Earlier, Margaret kayaked across the lagoon to pick up fresh oysters. Manka's, recently visited by the Prince of Wales and Duchess of Cornwall, was named the best restaurant in the United States by the *Telegraph London*.

The Snap of White (*opposite*) An elaborate faience stove, found in the South of France, is a focal point in Myra Hoefer's living room. The verdant garden outside her windows includes Iceberg roses, a French-inspired iron trellis that supports roses and ivy, and a series of charming topiaries.

In Chalk Hill, Kaye Heafey is cutting long stems of clematis. For the moment all that exists are the caress of the sun on the nape of her neck, the mysteries hidden in each tendril of clematis vine, and the simple glory of this moment. Kaye has perfected field-growing more than two hundred varieties of clematis. Her superbly tended Chalk Hill Clematis farm also nurtures heirloom English roses and fragrant flowering shrubs. Kaye and her husband, Richard, an ethics professor, are bottling extra-virgin olive oil pressed from olives grown on their remote property. With chef Paul Bertolli they are also crafting a beautifully balanced, delicately sweet *aceto balsamico*, which enhances a lovely afternoon salad of tender arugala leaves, crisp crescents of baby romaine leaves, and Green Zebra tomatoes.

North of Calistoga in his Gustavian pavilion, artist Ira Yeager sits on his balcony reading a book about late-eighteenth-century France and gazing out over gnarled vines to a hazy distance of madrones and manzanitas.

Baroque patterns of Bach's *Goldberg Variations* whirl through the air. Arpeggios are intertwined with the soft whirr of hummingbirds. Feasting on jasmine blossoms, the iridescent birds weave intricate arcs and fly into the blue yonder.

In a remote corner where Mendocino County, Lake County, and Sonoma County collide, Denise Hale is heading for the hills in her yellow jeep, checking out the water supplies for her cattle. Her dogs, Ming and Angel, have stayed at home in the cool shade of the brick terrace.

Later they will play, and perhaps splash in the pool. High on a hidden hillside above Pebble Beach, an art connoisseur has designed a modernist retreat. Garden designers and architects visit from around the world, drawn to her environmental concepts and planet-healthy garden plan.

A love of nature and the desire to dig in the earth and walk among centuries-old California native oaks can overpower even the most ardent city dweller.

For the moment these designers, gardeners, artists, and chefs have erased the memory of any world beyond their emerald borders, and all they imagine is another day, another week, in these Elysian fields.

In the warm, green heart of St. Helena, Martha Angus spends a rare lazy day on her terrace. The afternoon is imbued with the sharp fragrance of eucalyptus. And along the winding roads through the Russian River Valley, Richard Anderson's house is hidden among the redwoods, where nature almost seems to have gained the upper hand.

Fortunate indeed are those who spend their lives, or weekends and holidays, in the California countryside, certain of the stars that shower the night with silk, and confident of the glide of seasons, one to another.

I lived in my own childhood paradise among the foothills of the Southern Alps in the remote South Island of New Zealand, with apple blossom–scented springtimes, snow-melt rivers for summer swimming, miles of poplar-framed fields, and days of sacred solitude.

In my memory, I climb to the tops of pine trees. Perched among the sticky branches, my hair spiked with pine needles, I am no longer earthbound. The curve of the horizon twists and rolls as wind buffets the trees.

Back down to earth from my sylvan escape, I adjust my inner compass and listen to the sibilant sounds of my footsteps through the long grass to reassure myself of my safe return.

I pick up a sketchbook and retreat to the garden to draw and paint once-more ideal worlds. I daydream. The countryside does not demand that we fill our days and our minds with ambitious plans. We can depart from the created world, slipping into an Edenic grace.

In the Delta, pear farmer Chiles Wilson contemplates his orchard, and in Mill Valley Paul Vincent Wiseman navigates his living room through ziggurats of rare books. In the Anderson Valley, Jed Pogran plants saplings, and in her lavish corner of the Napa Valley, Maria Manetti Farrow appraises her fragrant pink roses.

In the country, self-expression is in the air. In Healdsburg, Myra Hoefer's Ivy House windows are dressed in luscious silk curtains, as elegant as classic Balenciaga ballgowns. Michael Vanderbyl and Anna Hernandez pour a glass or two of Cabernet Sauvignon and toast their wedding anniversary. Dave de Mattei and Patrick Wade invite dinner guests to walk outside and stargaze over the Mayacamas Range.

Brunno and Urannia Ristow build a duck pond near their house and feed migrating Canadian geese with vitamin-fortified cracked corn.

Days and star-spangled nights in the California countryside are waiting to be created and savored. ❧

French Flavor (above) In San Francisco interior designer Steven Volpe's decor, a hammered architectural fragment found in Paris has been mounted as a dramatic lamp. This living room/media room is in a house in Hillsborough. The nineteenth-century bas-relief paper plaques are by Marie Pierre Jaudel. A series of eighteenth-century celadon urns are from Antonio's Antiques, San Francisco.

California

CLASSICS

———

Le monde s'endort dans une chaude lumière. Là, tout n'est
qu'ordre et beauté, luxe, calme et volupté.

The world falls asleep in a drowsy light. There, all is order
and beauty, luxury, tranquility, and exquisite pleasure.

❧

CHARLES BAUDELAIRE [1821–1867]
from *"L'Invitation au Voyage"*
("Invitation to the Voyage"),
Les Fleurs du Mal

COUNTRY SPLENDOR

Interior designer ANN GETTY's *elegant villa among the walnut groves in Wheatland, Yuba County*

———

WHEN ANN GETTY WAS TWELVE, HER FATHER ACQUIRED WALNUT AND PEACH ORCHARDS OUTSIDE THE SMALL AGRICULTURAL TOWN OF WHEATLAND, IN NORTHERN CALIFORNIA. THE FAMILY MOVED TO THIS LUSH FARMLAND NEAR THE BEAR AND SACRAMENTO RIVERS.

There in Yuba County Ann and her brothers enjoyed an idyllic childhood. She rode her bicycle along country roads framed by tall walnut trees, rode her horse to the river to join her brothers for a swim, or helped with the harvests.

"We grew peaches and several varieties of walnuts, and life was very healthy and carefree out in the country-side," recalled Getty, who also spent winters skiing in the nearby Sierra Nevada.

Getty now lives in San Francisco, where ten years ago she founded her interior design company, Ann Getty & Associates. Five years ago she started Ann Getty House, to design and produce collections of upholstered furniture in addition to fine reproduction furniture and accessories, based on her museum-worthy collections of English and French antiques and Chinese porcelains.

Now with company offices in the Presidio, a former army headquarters overlooking San Francisco Bay, Ann Getty recently began producing a fabric collection based on her extensive collections of antique textiles, including Indian hand-printed cottons and rare silk brocades woven in Lyon, France.

The Ann Getty House collection, with more than seventy pieces in its line, is now available for custom orders and is represented in to-the-trade showrooms in California, New York, and Florida.

"I've been interested in decoration and antiques most of my life," said Getty, sitting in the malachite-green dining room of her city house. "My mother had a great sense of elegance and style, so I was exposed to fashion and design, even though Wheatland seemed quite remote, and we were living in the middle of a farming region."

Mediterranean Inspiration (opposite) Ann Getty has remodeled and enlarged her Wheatland house over the last decade. Using Spanish and Italian country villas as templates, she added shady loggias to provide escape from the summer heat. Gardeners maintain the parterres and lavish plantings of Iceberg roses, pink and white geraniums, blue and white agapanthus, jasmine, and alyssum and trailing ivy, which thrive even when the temperature hovers around 98 degrees for days on end.

Escape to the Country *(left, above, and right)* Ann Getty's gardens are planted to remain colorful and textured throughout the year. Blue-and-white bearded irises provide a delicate wash of color in the spring, and tall blue agapanthus bloom in the parterres close to the loggias most of the summer. Surrounding the house are a series of cutting gardens, a broad shaded lawn on which Getty has clustered a collection of children's playhouses from around the world (a Polynesian thatched hut, a Bavarian folly, a charming Swiss cottage), as well as a swimming pool, guesthouses, and barns.

Rich in Detail *(above and opposite)* As an interior and furniture designer, Ann Getty takes great pleasure in layering and enriching her rooms. In the Wheatland living room, which opens to a loggia and sunny lawns and gardens, she has covered her walls with eight English chinoiserie panels, circa 1740, as well as faux-oak veined and gilded crown moldings, trim, and panels. The delicately painted oak panels have gold-leaf knots. The lavish curtains, in the bishop sleeve manner, are in three shades of Indian silk. A pair of George I gilded armchairs are covered in antique blue silk damask. Getty has embellished the walls with a pair of George II tree-form wall sconces, circa 1760, with Chinese porcelain saints as well as gilded girandoles. The corner banquette, crafted by Hildebrand Design, San Francisco, is covered in tiger-striped silk velvet woven by Bevilacqua, Venice.

After marrying Gordon Getty, a composer, she worked closely with New York interior designers "Sister" Parish and Albert Hadley to decorate the family's houses and apartments, and later she studied paleoanthropology at Berkeley. For several years, Getty spent months at a time on archaeological digs in Ethiopia, Sicily, and Greece. Studying and excavating classical architecture gave her a heightened sense of proportion, line, balance, and scale in design, she says.

Today Getty is fully immersed in her design work. She frequently flies in her jet to Shanghai, where she is completing residential projects, to Jaipur, India, to commission embroideries and furniture, or to Moscow to enjoy performances of her husband's operas.

When Ann Getty takes a moment to sip a demitasse in her mirrored dining room, with its panoramic view of San Francisco Bay, she's surrounded by museum-quality antiques and a superb art collection that includes romantic Utrillo landscapes, a Monet, and sexy Balthus portraits.

"I have to laugh when I'm described as a socialite," she said, displaying some new linen fabrics. "I'm totally involved in my work. I go out once a month only to maintain my so-called socialite status."

She's the first to arrive most mornings at the atelier, where she checks curtains and drawings and plans interiors for her devoted clients and sketches additions to her furniture line. Her collection includes her best-selling hand-carved Venus chair, which has gilt bronze ornamentation and a hand-carved Botticelli-style scallop-shell back.

"I'm totally hands-on," she noted. "For my living room, I stitched pillows and repaired antique embroideries. I've been very practical since I was a girl, driving tractors, fixing electrical wiring, working in the orchards."

Her roster of clients—young San Francisco families, social-register couples, and style-conscious entrepreneurs—is growing, but this is no overnight success. She credits her demanding studies at UC Berkeley with giving her a fine sense of color and proportion and helping her visualize decor. For more than forty years, she's been at the center of the international art and antiques world, first as a student and later as a serious buyer at auctions.

"I learned many of the finer points of decorating from 'Sister' Parish and Albert Hadley of Parish-Hadley, as well as from John Stefanidis, who decorated my guest rooms," said Ann. "I worked closely with the California firm Leavitt-Weaver and learned about the design profession from them as well."

Twelve years ago, Ann Getty began a large-scale redecoration of the Pacific Heights house where she lives with her husband, Gordon. It was built in 1906 to a classic design by architect Willis Polk and offers an entry hall with collections as opulent as those found in any London museum.

The Gettys, generous philanthropists, often entertain an international retinue of cultural and political figures.

Seven years ago Ann also undertook the renovation and restoration of her family's house in Wheatland, where her brothers still maintain walnut orchards. At auctions in New York and London, she acquired furniture from the great English country houses— Badminton House, Ditchley Park. Unable to collect French antiques (the Getty Museum was in an acquisition phase, and her budget was not large enough to bid against the institution, she said), she gathered George II gilded chairs, dramatic Anglo-Indian beds inlaid with mother-of-pearl, and porcelain and ormolu *objets*.

"I love the heft and boldness of English antiques," said Getty, who is also a jewelry designer and a champion of arts education.

In Paris she scooped up vivid eighteenth-century silk brocades for pillows. From the estate of Rudolf Nureyev she acquired velvet patchwork textiles, which she made into dramatic curtains.

"This is the ornate look I love for myself, but I don't impose it on my clients," she noted. "My work is not all over-the-top design. For clients, I want rooms that reflect their style."

Sumptuous Dreams (opposite) Ann Getty's bedroom suite, which overlooks a dreamy rose garden, is enriched by antiques from a lifetime of collecting. The bed is a George III painted and parcel gilt four-poster style, late eighteenth century, dressed in embroidered silks from Old World Weavers. The pale blue silk is from Silk Trading Company. The Russian rug, circa 1835, was acquired from the Luttrellstown Castle auction. Getty is particularly fond of large-scale eighteenth-century chairs and has a museum-worthy collection in the Wheatland house, as well as in her San Francisco residence. This pair of painted and gilded scroll-arm Regency chairs, attributed to Thomas Hope, are upholstered in fragments of silk brocade, circa 1780, woven in Lyon. The interior design is by Ann Getty, Ann Getty & Associates, San Francisco.

A Passage to India *(above and opposite)* Ann Getty takes friends and family on a magical mystery tour of India in the Anglo-Indian guest suite. Capturing the delights of Mogul India, a nineteenth-century painted metal and wood chest depicts sari-clad women dancing and tempting peacocks with pomegranates and figures taking the night air on an ornate terrace. Walls are covered in Rosemount cotton by Marvic, London. The same cotton was used for balloon shades.

The nineteenth-century faux-bamboo beds inspired the door surrounds, trim, and crown molding in a superbly proportioned faux bamboo. The mid-nineteenth-century Indian portraits are reverse painting on glass *(verre églomisé)*. The rug is a rare nineteenth-century Louis Philippe needlepoint, circa 1840, acquired in London. An antique ivory temple-shaped box and a mother-of-pearl ornamented desk enhance the Indian mood.

After a day of swimming or an evening of bowling in the Sierra foothills refuge, guests as well as grandchildren can often be found sprawled on silken sofas, and friends curled up to sip champagne on chairs covered with luscious handwoven Venetian silk velvets and Lyon silk-brocade fragments.

In the city, a quartet of Canaletto paintings hovers above a gilded console table in the music room, a theatrical stage for family celebrations. A Sèvres porcelain table commissioned by Napoleon (its pair is installed in Buckingham Palace) stands in a corner. Gilded benches and tables from Spencer House, and a silk-upholstered glass chair with the look of carved crystal, all demonstrate Getty's original eye.

In the country, a series of antique Chinese porcelain saint figures, each delicately detailed and colored, stands on a carved and gilded tree of life, which is mounted on a lacquered and gilded chinoiserie panel on a living room wall.

While Getty often designs practical rooms for young families, her own rooms glow with baroque splendor. Blossoms, birds, and butterflies painted on pale blue Chinese silk panels glimmer on the walls of a bedroom. Silken curtains cascade about a carved and gilded antique four-poster bed.

"Designing is a minor art, but such a pretty one," mused Ann, as she glanced over her living room. "I love to create interiors that please the eye. Beauty can be so uplifting." ❧

Even among this grandeur, there are quiet corners for an afternoon tête-à-tête overlooking the Palace of Fine Arts in the city and the walnut groves near Wheatland.

Her gracious rooms in city and country, with tufted sofas and chairs covered in plum-colored velvets, banquettes lavished with tiger-striped Bevilacqua silk velvets, and pillows gleaming with gold-threaded silks, are at once exotic, dazzling, and comfortable.

Bedrooms and guest rooms in both Wheatland and Pacific Heights are bewitching. In the country, an Anglo-Indian guest suite with mother-of-pearl inlaid desks and bamboo beds feels like a retreat in a Jodhpur palace.

WEEKEND ESCAPE ROUTE

DENISE HALE's *country hacienda east of Cloverdale*

———

WHEN DENISE HALE FIRST VISITED THE H-E RANCH, EAST OF CLOVERDALE, IN APRIL 1969, SHE FOUND THE HACIENDA-STYLE RESIDENCE GLOOMY, AND FAR FROM THE GLAMOROUS HIDEOUT SHE HAD IMAGINED. "LATER I FELL IN LOVE WITH IT, BUT that first time I thought it was the most depressing house I'd ever seen," recalled Hale, who lives in a chic art-filled apartment on Russian Hill.

Over the next two decades, the ranch became a great escape for Denise and her husband, Prentis Cobb Hale. The adobe house had been built in the fifties, to be used for only two months a year, as a hunting retreat. Hale had her own vision for the interior.

"On a visit to an English country house when I was nineteen, I had seen the most beautiful interiors with polished wood floors, fires blazing, fresh flowers, silver candelabra, all in a rustic setting, all very comfortable and elegant," said Hale. "It was the most beautiful and inviting house I'd ever seen, and I thought maybe one day, I could have that."

Over the years, she has imbued the rooms of the ranch with European style and Frette embroidered sheets, antique Persian rugs, marble obelisks from Florence, stacks of books everywhere, large-scale contemporary paintings, silver candelabra, fresh roses from her garden, and even the blazing fires and waxed floors reminiscent of the inviting English country house she remembered so vividly.

Denise is known to social-column readers and to *Vanity Fair* magazine subscribers as San Francisco's most famous truly glamorous jet-setter.

A close friend of kings and queens and princes and princesses, current and exiled, and best pal of social swans too numerous to mention, Denise glides effortlessly and glamorously from gala balls to private lunches. From palaces and palazzi, and on to *intime* weekends with famous (and notorious) actors, she's also the A-list guest and friend of best-selling authors, dukes and duchesses, leading dermatologists, city honchos, fashion designers, editors, and the talented and witty around the world.

California Latitudes (opposite) The view south across the hills of the H-E Ranch.

Into the Green *(above)* Exterior of the ranch house.

Speaking French *(left)* Hermès porcelain plates and a matching Hermès teapot and place mats, in a signature setting with carved Chinese jade bowls and spoons, and chopsticks.

Around the World and Back *(right)* At one end of the living room—traversed through ziggurats of art and history volumes—is a gathering of antiques and objects from travels far and abroad. The gilt candlesticks are treasures from one of many visits to Rajasthan, India. Animal skins from Africa, a 19th-century English chair, and a chinoiserie chest from Denise Hale's apartment in Rome are brought into the present with a contemporary oil painting.

A View from the Terrace (*left*) In summer, cocktails, informal dinners, and beautiful lunches prepared by assistant/chef Ted Hiscox are enjoyed on the terrace. Denise Hale designed the terrace with a Persian carpet and billowing cotton canvas curtains, inspired by La Fiorentina, on the French Riviera. The hydrangeas are from Jerry Bolduan's Green Valley Growers. The company, based in Northern California, grows more than eighty-five varieties of hydrangea.

Her glamour—and longtime essence of cool—precedes her, and she's greeted by name by maître d's and longtime fans from Paris to Palm Beach. A supporter of the San Francisco–based Delancey Street Foundation, she is recognized far from home base while touring Angkor Wat, even while slipping semi-incognito into the Ritz-Carlton hotel in Shanghai. "It's Denise Hale" (no explanation required).

At lunch at the Voltaire in Paris, the suave Prince Michael of Greece and his lovely wife will make a beeline to greet the silver-haired beauty. "She knows everyone, and everyone knows her," whispered an admirer.

But the surprise is that when her plane lands back in California, she often prefers to be alone, escaping to her eight-thousand-cattle ranch in the hills near the Mendocino County border.

"I'm an enigma to many people," said Hale. "I grew up in Europe, I fled certain death in Yugoslavia, so I think differently. I love to have a great social life, but I also value solitude, being with one or two superclose friends. I love to be alone at the ranch."

Her life can be one of extremes.

"I am in some ways the little girl from Belgrade whose grandparents exposed me to an international life," she said. "I went to Truman Capote's Black and White Ball, and Baron Alexis de Redé's Orientalist Ball in Paris, and I adore that glamour. Being alone in the California country air, with my new German shepherd puppies or feeding my wild ducks, is a great luxury."

Sparking the Conversations *(above and opposite)* Hale loves to travel, and the table reflects her international treasures. Silver temples from Pagan in Myanmar and English silver chargers, from 1740, are arranged with garden roses on a *pietra dura* dining table custom-made in Agra, India.

She's chic, she's classic, and Hale has been, seemingly effortlessly, in the fashion style leaders' Hall of Fame since she was in her early twenties when she first hit New York's social pages. (El Morocco, anyone?)

Today her favorite designers are Gianfranco Ferre and Ralph Rucci. Even in the country she looks elegant, dressed in monogrammed petit-point loafers, cream gabardine slacks, and a white Chanel T-shirt.

"I've led a privileged life," she noted. "I've been incredibly fortunate."

To add to the drama—and mystery, and perhaps her introspection—Hale escaped from war-torn Yugoslavia as a teenager, with her young cousin. A Royal Navy ship picked up the pair as they bobbed

about in a rowboat in the Adriatic Sea. Hale kept in touch with the captain of the ship, who saved her life, and still keeps his letters in an album.

Later, more happily, there was the high life in Rome, with husband number one, and in the sixties the chic movie scene in Los Angeles with husband number two, director Vincente Minnelli. Her love match with husband number three, Prentis Cobb Hale, has lasted more than twenty-seven years.

"Today I'm running a working cattle ranch," said Hale. "I'm learning on the job. It's a lot of work. I meet with the foreman and the cattlemen, and work in the garden. There is always so much to take care of.

"I have complete silence here," she said. "And I like the luxury and beauty here, just as I do in the city. We have dinner on eighteenth-century silver plates; we have Hermès towels on the terrace. I love understated things."

The shady terrace overlooking the pool is decorated with Persian rugs, canvas curtains inspired by La Fiorentina, and masses of hydrangeas grown by her great friend, Jerry Bolduan of Green Valley Growers in Sebastopol.

"I found nirvana at the ranch," said Hale. "Once I'm up there, I never want to leave." ❧

Fragrant Days (*left and opposite*) Jasmine flourishes on the pool terrace and fills the air with scent. Swimmers in the sunlit pool drift back and forth, thinking sweet thoughts, certainly, and taking a perfumed cool dip on a hot afternoon before picking up a book and reading into the twilight.

Shades of Summer *(right)* Hale dreamed up
a shaded pool terrace with the style of Capri
and Cap d'Antibes, but set in the rugged
hills west of Cloverdale, California. The
style: cushions striped in taupe and natural
off-white, trophies of long-ago safaris on the
walls, Perrier-Jouët champagne chilling in a
Christofle cooler, and lots of Hermès towels
for devoted swimmers. Friends from around
the world lap it up.

THE LUXURY OF SILENCE AND SECLUSION

The Wiseman Group *and* Timothy Gemmill *create
a Spanish Colonial Revival house in Dry Creek Valley*

———

SAN FRANCISCO INTERIOR DESIGNER PAUL VINCENT WISEMAN AND HIS TEAM AT THE WISEMAN GROUP HAD WORKED ON RESIDENTIAL PROJECTS WITH JAY AND KÄREN ABBE FOR SOME YEARS, SO WHEN THE COUPLE ACQUIRED A HOUSE ON 160 acres in Dry Creek Valley, a noted wine appellation near Healdsburg, it was natural that Wiseman would be consulted.

"We drove up to the house for a site inspection," recalled Joseph Matzo, senior design principal with the firm. "Jay Abbe, who pilots his own plane, told us that his children had flown the coop, the family dog had died, and that they needed a new house, a fresh start, a grown-ups' house."

Architect Timothy Gemmill, of the San Francisco–based Gemmill Design Architecture & Interiors, was introduced to the owners by The Wiseman Group.

The project began as a remodel. The owners hoped that with some modification, and elegant new interiors by The Wiseman Group, the existing house would feel spacious, rich in detail, entirely comfortable, and at home in the landscape. "I wanted the house to interact strongly with the outdoors without losing the experience of gracious traditional interior spaces," said Gemmill. "That goal became a driving force throughout the development of the architectural design."

It was soon apparent to the owners, the interior design firm, and the architect that the existing house, built in the seventies, would not suit the couple's requirements over the years.

The Spanish Colonial and Mediterranean architectural approach, done with a light hand, they decided, would lend itself to many of the architect's and the interior designers' inventive and playful ideas.

California History (opposite) San Francisco architect Timothy Gemmill looked to Mission Revival and Spanish Colonial Revival architecture as a reference for the Healdsburg-area house, which overlooks vineyards. The walls are made of Durisol, a twelve-inch-thick block made from wood chips and glue, stacked by a stonemason, and filled with concrete and rebar. This material gives the house a solid, thick wall and performs similarly to adobe, according to the architect. The contractor was Alex Hunt, Monsoon Construction.

"It's a great concept to work with because there are not a lot of rules for an architect to be concerned with," said Gemmill. "The concept was somewhat open to interpretation. The historic buildings in the Presidio, a former army base in San Francisco near the Golden Gate Bridge, were a great resource for Spanish Colonial influences. I took many walks around those buildings with my sketch pad."

The style of the house largely dictated the materials: thick plaster walls, a clay tile roof with wood, steel-framed windows and doors, and iron detail.

"I made a deliberate effort to prevent any connotation of 'Tuscan villa' pastiche architecture, which has become such a cliché in California," noted the architect. "Going back to European references, the design draws more from provincial Andalusian examples. But more important is the unique architectural history of California, with its Spanish Colonial and Mission-style examples."

The Wiseman Group and their clients maintained a strict goal to use only quality materials, such as stone, recycled old-growth redwood, and rich but unpretentious silks, linens, cottons, and wools for the upholstery and furnishings. The color palette would include ocher, terracotta, taupe, lichen, soft gray, ivory, and rose madder.

"Our firm tends to work in a very controlled, understated palette, and we refined the Abbes' color palette so that it did not call attention to itself and felt natural to that location," said Matzo. "We didn't cover the windows with any fabrics or shades. You can see the vineyards and the pond from most rooms."

Sense of Ease (left and opposite) The living room architecture and decor, antiques and art, are so well integrated and balanced that they feel as if they have been there for decades, not a mere few years. The intricate beamed ceiling, with massive bracketed trusses, purlins, and rafters, was crafted using recycled old-growth redwood. Large-scale furniture includes a sofa made by Fitzgerald to The Wiseman Group's design, and chairs and an ottoman by Rose Tarlow. The occasional tables are also by Rose Tarlow Melrose House. The Huntington floor lamps were designed by The Wiseman Group and crafted by Phoenix Day. Walls are integral-color plaster. A tall inlaid secretary in the Italian style was crafted by C. Mariani, San Francisco. The carpet is by V'Soske. Interior design is by Joseph Matzo and James Hunter, The Wiseman Group.

Summer Garden Roses (above and opposite) The roses were picked from the Abbes' garden. On the table is an antique surveyor's transit from Rue de Grenelle, an antique gallery in San Francisco. The window seat cantilevers out from the floor of the massive living room, affording views across ponds and meadows to clouds of steam from far-off geysers to the north. The walnut occasional tables are by Sir Edwin Lutyens, a favorite architect of Paul Vincent Wiseman. The V'Soske carpet was designed by The Wiseman Group. The color scheme was influenced by the natural materials found on the site. Kären Abbe collected lichen, moss-covered rocks, feathers, leaves, bark, pinecones, weeds, and dry grasses and brought them to an early meeting with the interior designers, who based their selection of fabrics, patterns, colors, and weaves on that inspiration.

The architectural color palette was extremely important in this respect. The roof tiles were selected in dark and light brown and tan tones. It was critical that no Tuscan-influenced red or orange tones be used. The plaster color is a subdued off-white, which relates closely to the white lime washes seen in the early California Spanish Colonial houses. Gemmill said it was equally challenging not to create a cliché Spanish Colonial–style house.

"The client had expressed an interest in using glazed terra-cotta floor tiles on the interior, and red brick pavers on the exterior," he noted. "While those materials are extremely common in this style of house, it really did feel like a cliché. The house is not a literal interpretation of any specific style."

The remodel and redesign took almost four years, including more than a year for design and drawings prior to construction, and over two years in construction and the completion and fine-tuning of the interiors.

For stylistic references Gemmill spent months on research, often focusing on Spanish Colonial architecture built in California between 1915 and 1930.

"These buildings were very much influenced by the earlier Spanish Colonial buildings, and the original missions and adobes," said Gemmill. "The two California architects whose work I constantly studied and drew from throughout the design process were Wallace Neff and George Washington Smith. They were both thoroughly familiar with the farmhouses of Andalusia and simpler rural forms of Spanish architecture, which can be seen in their architecture."

A Room for All Seasons (right) The kitchen/
family room includes a large open cooking
center, equipped with a Viking range and
custom side cabinets, as well as a spacious
sitting and dining area. The cooking/serving
island was crafted from a large oak tree on
the property that fell during a storm. Pendant
lighting and sconces are by Paul Ferrante.
The room also opens onto an enclosed
courtyard, right, where the family can dine
in summer. Rose Tarlow Melrose House
Pemberton chairs and an ottoman give
the room a sense of scale and comfort.

A Room with a View *(this page and opposite)* As the Abbes were initiating the process of evolving a rather ordinary house on their property into a highly individual and richly detailed new residence, Jay Abbe and contractor Alex Hunt discovered an abandoned mill with numerous old-growth logs that had been left behind. The owner set up his own sawmill on the spot and converted the garage into a kiln to dry the cut wood. This old-growth wood was used to great effect in the ceiling of the upstairs bathroom. Steel windows open to the view over vineyards and golden summer meadows. Marble, stone, and mosaic are in taupe, ivory, gray, and beige tones to showcase the ceiling and the view. The soaking tub was raised so that bathing could include a view of the seasonal panorama. The windows were made by Architectural Iron Works in Southern California.

In the end, the simple "remodel" became a much more complex and polished project, one resulting in a handsome house with no compromises.

"I'm very pleased with the multifaceted qualities of the house," said the architect. "The bold scale of the architecture blends with the house's casual character, and I like the basic simplicity contrasted against the finely articulated detail and the variety of the rooms and spaces."

Gemmill's favorite aspect of the house is the sequence of spaces and the connection from one room to the other.

For The Wiseman Group, taking each step with their clients and exceeding their expectations made this an extremely satisfying project.

"We enjoyed incorporating stone, old-growth redwood, plaster, tile, and metal to create a residence that will age gracefully and look even better and richer over time," said Matzo.

"We provided the most luxurious and comfortable furniture," said the designer. "In the end it's the seclusion that makes it wonderful. They are surrounded by the most beautiful landscape, the fresh country air, and the silence. We gave them the setting in which to enjoy it all." ❧

SEPARATE LATITUDES

MYRA HOEFER's Paris-influenced Ivy House in Healdsburg

———

INTERIOR DESIGNER MYRA HOEFER LIVES IN AN ELEGANT AND EXTRAORDINARILY ROMANTIC HOUSE IN THE CENTER OF THE TOWN OF HEALDSBURG, IN SONOMA COUNTY, ABOUT AN HOUR'S DRIVE NORTH OF THE GOLDEN GATE BRIDGE. HOEFER has been an ardent Francophile since she was a young girl growing up in Vancouver. Perhaps in her studies she came upon French author Honoré de Balzac's statement "Whoever does not visit Paris regularly will never be elegant."

Holidays in the south of France, long summer vacations in Paris, and design projects on the Left Bank increased her love and admiration of all things French. Now she is living her own French dream, with a house in Healdsburg and an apartment and atelier in Paris, which she visits often.

Hoefer's house in Healdsburg, just a hop and a skip from her design store, 21 Arrondissement, is named the Ivy House, for the drifting curtains of Virginia creeper and Boston ivy that drape the exterior all summer and give the residence a mysterious eighteenth-century Trianon-in-the-park feeling. Even the parterre in front has swags of ivy creeping along iron trellises fashioned after traditional designs Hoefer had seen at L'Isle-sur-la-Sorgue while on an antiques quest in the south of France.

The designer discovered the Ivy House a decade ago. It had previously been the residence of a piano teacher and her two grand pianos, all very Proust.

"When I moved in, I realized the front windows were rather visible to the street, so we built brick and plaster walls in front to create privacy," said Hoefer. "We planted an all-white garden with Iceberg roses, Japanese anemones, espaliered heirloom apple trees, clipped ivy in old French terra-cotta pots, Greek amphorae, and antique French garden furniture. We sometimes sit out there to enjoy the beautiful summer weather and sip a glass of wine, perhaps enjoy afternoon tea."

Bon Appétit (opposite) At one end of the large living room, interior designer Myra Hoefer has placed a white-painted Astier de Villatte dining table, which she also uses for client meetings. The French chairs are modern reproductions of a classic Louis XVI design by the Paris-based company Moissonnier. The oil painting, entitled *Aeriae*, by Wade Hoefer, was painted in honor of Myra Hoefer. The floor is covered in sea-grass matting.

The interior decor of the Ivy House is Hoefer's homage to Paris.

With its pale oyster-colored silk taffeta curtains, Louis Seize–style chairs, and Mme de Pompadour–style slipper chairs upholstered in silk velvet, her living room could be a salon in the Sixteenth Arrondissement.

She dressed the large windows with wood-slat venetian blinds and painted the plaster walls pale lichen.

"I like these pale, pale colors because they can read soft celadon or off-white or pale blue in different lights during the day. Lichen and oyster are also a perfect neutral background for changing decor," said Hoefer.

Her windows are dressed in silk taffeta curtains interlined and backed with natural jute hopsacking. "The jute is very practical," said Hoefer. "It makes the silk impervious to the sun and looks quite rustic when viewed from the garden."

The jute also gives the silk, by Silk Trading Company, the body and sway of a crinoline.

"I like the combination of 'rich and poor' fabrics, a very French style statement," said Hoefer.

Classic French style is opulent, but always apparent is an appreciation of the irony and contrast of a rich and refined silk with a material that's quite humble, like handwoven linen or simple cotton muslin.

The floors of all Ivy House rooms are covered in sea-grass matting, a practical choice, since Hoefer lives there with her two beloved Jack Russell terriers that also love to pose in photographs. Mr. Wick from County Wicklow and Lady Gittisham from Devon have their run of the house and love to sleep on the silk pillows.

Paris is yesterday and today and tomorrow for Hoefer, so ardent is her desire to immerse herself in the antiques stores, the flea markets, the restaurants, and her favorite furniture stores.

She alights from the plane with just a lightweight carry-on bag and heads for her luminous second-floor apartment two blocks from the historic Place des Vosges. Her Marais neighborhood, with its grand mansions and museums, has escaped any modernization, and traffic sounds and business bustle seem far away.

Hoefer's five-hundred-square-foot retreat, which overlooks a cobblestone courtyard that dates back to the seventeenth century, is situated in a former hayloft above garage spaces that once sheltered horses and carriages.

She loves her quiet neighborhood so much that she has now set up an office in a sunny corner of her courtyard, and she keeps a large design atelier nearby.

Paris Calling (opposite) The curvy sofa was crafted by Michael Taylor · Designs after an original design by Syrie Maugham. Hoefer had it covered in pale taupe linen velvet from the Silk Trading Company. The hand-stenciled silk pillows are by Cary Nowell, a Ross, California, designer.

"Paris is the most beautiful city in the world, and I travel there on business at least six or eight times a year," said Hoefer. "I had always wanted an apartment so that I would feel part of the life and fabric of the city and not seem like a visitor. I am inspired by the historic limestone buildings, the classic Paris architecture, the great variety of antiques, the creative people, and the range of stylish decor. Rooms in Paris feel soulful, and rich in history. I feel at peace and inspired when I'm in my apartment. I return to California full of new ideas, truly energized and excited about decorating."

Finding her one-bedroom apartment and setting up shop in Paris were the result of a series of fortunate and fateful events. First, a San Francisco friend inherited a Paris apartment near the Bastille eight years ago and asked Hoefer to decorate it. After the apartment was published, Sharyl Rupert, the founder/owner of Chez Vous, a Sausalito-based Paris apartment rental company, called and asked Hoefer to create new decor for a series of apartments in the Chez Vous portfolio.

Hoefer now has had a ten-year relationship with Chez Vous, decorating classic apartments on quiet, historic streets, courtyards, and squares. (Apartments may be viewed at chezvous.com.) For these apartments, she dreams up French-style rooms with an airy, light, California freshness.

"I take California to Paris, and bring Paris back to Healdsburg," said Hoefer. "After two or three design changes, I have lightened the Ivy House up with pale oyster/chalk silk, white-painted tables, and colors of the Parisian sky. My life is dedicated to beauty and design. I am truly fortunate. " ❧

Dining Light (opposite, top left) Hoefer has a particular talent for flower styling and often sources garden flowers from local growers. These branches of roses were from Chalk Hill Clematis in Healdsburg. The candlesticks and vase are from PS Italia, Healdsburg. Hoefer planned the large mirror, with its rough-hewn wood frame, to add light and dimension to this dining and meeting area of the living room.

Breakfast in Healdsburg (opposite, bottom left) Hovering over the breakfast room, which also serves as an impromptu office, is a framed antique travelers' folding map mounted on muslin depicting a bird's-eye view of 1908 Paris. On it Myra Hoefer has affixed stars locating apartments she designed on the Right Bank and the Left Bank for Chez Vous, the Sausalito-based Paris apartment rental company. The white-painted polygonal table is by Astier de Villatte. The bergère chair, covered in cotton muslin and trimmed with nail heads, is by Bergère de Marquis, a Paris furniture company. The wall is plastered in a rich mottled marigold/Naples yellow that Hoefer called "Napoleon's gold," since it was a favorite of the emperor.

Into the Clouds (opposite, top right) Artist Wade Hoefer created the virtuoso painting of clouds that hangs on the living room wall. Myra had the pair of club chairs covered in the same linen velvet as the sofa. The concrete table is by Buddy Rhodes. The gilded thorny rose branch amphora lamp is by Patrick Guffraz for Lieux. The lamp, with its classic form and poetic branch, is a delicate reference to the French love of wit, classic antiquity, and inventive contemporary design that give a discreet nod to neoclassicism.

French Toast (opposite, bottom right) Hoefer is an enthusiastic and generous hostess who often invites friends and family to dinner. Her kitchen is dominated by an antique Irish cabinet on which she has crammed a collection of antique French porcelain, English pottery, Portuguese platters, and English ironstone tureens and bowls. The table and stools are Hoefer's design. "They're compact, but four people can gather around sipping champagne while I'm preparing hors d'oeuvres or making a salad," she said.

A SENSE OF PLACE

CHILES *and* LESLIE WILSON'*s farmhouse in Walnut Grove, the Delta*

———

PEAR FARMER CHILES WILSON AND SAN FRANCISCO INTERIOR DESIGNER PAUL VINCENT WISEMAN GREW UP TOGETHER IN THE RICHLY FERTILE FARMING COUNTRY NEAR WALNUT GROVE, WHERE THE SACRAMENTO AND SAN JOAQUIN RIVERS SPILL across the California plains from the Sierra Nevada. This agricultural region is one of the most productive in the world.

Wiseman, whose family has farmed in the Delta for almost a century, grew up on his family's pear farm just a mile from Wilson's pear orchards. The two men have remained great friends throughout their lives, even attending college in Tasmania together. Wilson named his first son Paul Vincent in honor of Wiseman.

When Wilson and his wife, Leslie, planned to build a new house among six hundred acres of pear orchards, it was Wiseman they consulted.

Wiseman, who founded his firm, The Wiseman Group, more than twenty-five years ago, commissioned San Francisco architect Kurt Melander to shape the family's headquarters, which would include a guesthouse and barn to form a compound among the orchards.

"There's a tradition of fine modern architecture in the region," noted Wiseman. "Influential architects like William Wurster and William Turnbull have designed houses in the Delta. The Wilson property is particularly striking, on an island formed by levees, and reached over five drawbridges." Melander looked to California's history but avoided theme architecture.

"The concept was a four-thousand-two-hundred-square-foot working farmhouse and guest accommodations for a family that includes four children," noted Melander. "The architecture would allude subtly to historic California farm compounds. We planned practical and rather Spartan concrete floors, corrugated steel roofs, cool plaster interior walls, minimal detailing and trim, and wood-frame windows, for an effect that is simultaneously rural and modern."

In Search of the Continuous Present (opposite) Inspired by the simple forms, natural materials, and finely crafted details of historic California farm compounds, San Francisco architect Kurt Melander, with colleagues Rebecca Katlin and Don Robb, designed an elegant country house in the California Delta. Pear trees, willows, redwoods, walnuts, figs, native oaks, and palm trees surround the residence.

Melander and Wiseman and their clients were also inspired by early California Mission architecture, and the twelve-inch-thick walls recall old adobe haciendas that dotted the countryside in the nineteenth century.

"I decided to pare down the lines to their purest possible essence," said Melander, who is originally from Minnesota. "I put style on the back burner. This is a house for children, for family pets. It had to tame the extremely hot summers and the cool, rainy winters that pear farming requires."

The house was designed to be very welcoming, featuring a central living room/dining room/kitchen with low-maintenance concrete floors. White-painted wood ceilings soar up to seventeen feet and are lit by six clerestory windows.

"The windows are double-hung and double glazed with redwood sashes," noted Melander.

"Architects have a tendency to overdetail," he said. "I wanted this house to be very reductive. The dance, for me, was to balance elegance and richness, not to embellish and dress it up, and certainly not to go in the direction of a Tuscan villa, the California country cliché. Our focus was to design for a specific place and time, this specific family. Decoration and richness would come from the details of the decor Paul and his design associate, Jessica Cornell, selected—paintings, carpets, the play of light, fabrics, and furniture—and views of the pear orchards through the seasons."

Harvest Time (left) Among pear varieties grown on the Wilsons' orchards are Bartletts, Seckels, Boscs, Red Euros, and the colorful Trouts with speckled skins that resemble New Zealand rainbow trout.

Home Is Where the Hearth Is (opposite) Soaring ceilings in the living room give a sense of lightness and ease to this family gathering place. Chairs and a sofa designed by The Wiseman Group and crafted by Richard Andronaco surround a table handcrafted from an antique Indonesian door. The custom-crafted light fixtures by California lighting designer Robert Truax sport Coraggio sheer linen shades. The rush carpet is Stark Carpet's Hyacinth. Shanghai-born Ning Hou, who has a studio in the historic California Delta town of Locke, painted the vibrant oil, which depicts an orchard in spring. Interior decor is by Paul Vincent Wiseman and Jessica Cornell, The Wiseman Group.

The materials and setting are exposed to the weather, and the architects and designers embraced the seasons.

"This is a house designed to mature gracefully," said Melander. "Rain will stain the exterior, and sun will fade the fir posts. The steel roof with get a little rusty, like a traditional farmhouse. Nature will soften it, in an artistic and attractive Andy Goldsworthy fashion. In decades, we will admire the nobility and patina of age. The house will survive beautifully in this superb natural setting."

Wiseman often visits the Wilsons, observing the house throughout the seasons.

"It's a very serene house," said the designer, known for superbly detailed rooms. "The landscape is so dramatic outside, so we kept fabrics, rush carpets, and furniture rather simple and sculptural, without the distraction of pattern. The walls are thick, and the rooms feel quiet and tranquil. My friends will be enjoying this house for many generations." ❧

Feast for the Eyes (opposite and left) The large dining table was custom-made for the Wilson family. Paul Vincent Wiseman selected the recycled teak slabs in Indonesia. The floor is solar-heated concrete, for easy maintenance and temperature control. The dining chairs by Janus et Cie have pillows by Glant and Rogers & Goffigon. Wiseman found the fifties vintage candlesticks in Hudson, New York. Nine-inch and twelve-inch baseboards are inset with concealed air-conditioning vents. The painting is by Ning Hou.

Beckoning Us Closer *(above and right)* Luxury is given more emphasis in the bedroom, with Rose Tarlow's Edwin chair upholstered in a Cowtan & Tout fabric. An antique desk by Therien & Co. and a chair by Dessin Fournir contrast with the pared-down architecture of the house. The bed is dressed in a quilt, shams, and skirt in Rogers & Goffigon cotton/linen. The Lutyens-style bench is from British Khaki. The painting is by Ning Hou.

California Sunshine *(above)* In the Delta, daytime heat often rises above 100 degrees in the summer months, so San Francisco architect Kurt Melander gave the house broad overhangs for all-day shade. The overhangs and rafters are supported by simple Douglas fir posts and beams that were left unsealed, to allow them to age naturally. Thick walls are finished in lime-stucco plaster. Four Munder Skiles Taconic chairs in sustainably harvested teak surround a table crafted from a salvaged Indonesian teak door.

Lyrical Silhouettes *(opposite)* The chaises longues are by John Danzer for Munder Skiles. On a clear day, Mt. Diablo is visible to the south across the pear trees.

COUNTRY PLEASURES, COUNTRY STYLE

LESLIE RUDD's *private headquarters with interior design by* STEVEN VOLPE, *Rudd Winery, Oakville, Napa Valley*

———

SAN FRANCISCO INTERIOR DESIGNER STEVEN VOLPE IS ONE OF THE TOP WEST COAST DESIGNERS, A PART OF THE TREND-SETTING AND ENERGETIC AND AMBITIOUS COTERIE REINVENTING THE WAY CALIFORNIANS LIVE. VOLPE, WHO spends much of his professional and private life in Paris, Antwerp, New York, and London on the hunt for off-beat antiques, rare photography, new design inspiration, and beautiful objects, has thrown out the California clichés and instead casts a most cosmopolitan eye over antiques, art, and decor.

After studying in Paris, Volpe founded Steven Volpe Design in San Francisco some fifteen years ago; he then went on to found Hedge with his business partner, Roth Martin. Hedge has a chic antiques and fine furniture gallery on Gold Street in San Francisco, and sells both luxurious handcrafted interpretations of classic designs as well as limited-edition, custom-crafted forties, fifties, sixties, and seventies French, English, and American furniture, lighting, accessories, and contemporary art and decor.

It was not surprising that Leslie Rudd, a highly successful food and wine entrepreneur and talent spotter, would commission Steven Volpe to design both his San Francisco pied-à-terre and the elegant interiors of his winery.

Rudd, who acquired Dean & Deluca, an epicurean food company, in 1996, is a partner in Press Restaurant in the Napa Valley and the owner of Standard Beverage Corporation, based in Wichita, Kansas. He is intrigued by luxury products that carry pedigrees of Old World craftsmanship.

Under the guidance of Steven Volpe, the interior decor of his winery bears out his credo superbly.

Natural Colors *(opposite)* After he founded his sixty-four-acre Rudd Vineyards and Winery in Oakville in 1996, Leslie Rudd replanted forty-five acres of vineyards with close-spaced planting. With meticulous pruning, each vine is limited to ten buds against the typical thirty-six, to produce less fruit but more concentrated flavors. Rudd and his team built a new stone winery surrounded by gardens. Beneath it, subterranean caves, tasting rooms, and wine-making facilities were constructed. Architectural design by Lail Design Group, St. Helena. Landscape design by Roger Warner, Calistoga.

The International World of Wine The Rudd Winery building *(right)* is new, but Steven Volpe's decor gives it an air of tranquil history. Around the Louis XVI carved sandstone mantel *(opposite)*, he has gathered a pair of open-arm chairs in carved oak and woven leather, circa 1900, from the Galerie Jacques De Vos in Paris. A French convex mirror, circa 1860, is from March, San Francisco. The collection of neoclassical tole finials is from Hedge. Volpe found the papier-mâché masks by Robert Courtwright at the venerable Jean-Jacques Dutko gallery in Paris. In the sitting room *(above)*, a cocktail table of Belgian blue marble and old French oak is from Axel Vervoordt Kanaal, Antwerp. The Peking glass vases are by Robert Kuo. The tufted club chair by Steven Volpe Design is upholstered in chartreuse linen velvet from Lee Joffa. The walls are hand-troweled Marmorino Venetian plaster. Interior design is by Steven Volpe Design, San Francisco.

For Rudd's private quarters in the winery, Volpe traveled to Antwerp to find handsome antiques from noted *antiquaire* Axel Vervoordt, to Paris for antiques and art from Left Bank galleries and antiques dealers, and to his favorite antiques dealers and design showrooms in Los Angeles, New York, and San Francisco.

He contrasted a spectacular late-nineteenth-century Italian silversmith's worktable of painted pine and beech, from Axel Vervoordt, with natural Irish rush matting from the Waldo Collection. The rooms are enriched with a pair of fifties French nickel and verre églomisé tables, a *style* Rothschild sofa covered in Travers floral chintz and Bergamo glazed linen, and a collection of rare American and European books on wine.

One favorite source for Volpe is the Jean-Jacques Dutko gallery on the rue Bonaparte in Paris, where he acquired graphic papier-mâché masks by Robert Courtwright. At the nearby Galerie Jacques De Vos, he found a handsome pair of French open-arm chairs with woven leather seats, from the early twentieth century.

Volpe's style is to bring together contemporary art, such as a work on paper by David Tomb, with Japanese folk art carved and lacquered pug masks, patchwork flat-weave Turkish rugs, French forties andirons, French eighteenth-century mathematical textbooks with hand-bound parchment pages, and a bronze pendant lamp with a hand-stitched silk and parchment shade from Roman Thomas.

Leslie Rudd acquired his seventy acres of land in Oakville after inspiring visits to Bordeaux and Burgundy. The new Rudd winery, which appears quite modest, sits above twenty-two thousand square feet of subterranean caves, carved from a rocky hillside. There his grapes are fermented, and wines are aged in barrels. The caves are also a setting for private wine tasting, and an adjacent wine library where Rudd keeps his wine collection, used for comparative tastings.

The setting is an illustrious one. Nearby vineyards include Opus One, Harlan Estate, Screaming Eagle, and Silver Oak. The winery, which is open only by appointment, is located along the foothills of the Vaca Mountains on the eastern benchland of this world-renowned appellation. ❦

The Pleasures of Wine, Food, Great Style (opposite and above) At his Oakville winery, Leslie Rudd put together a fine team of wine industry veterans. As successive vintages draw raves, his executives, colleagues, and friends gather in the private dining rotunda to savor each bottle, along with seasonal cuisine crafted by his chef. Perhaps they will pour the complex, crisp, and herbal 2003 Napa Valley Sauvignon Blanc (described as "refreshing and attractive" by wine guru Robert M. Parker Jr.), which includes grapes grown in Oakville, Yountville, and nearby Rutherford. On the table, the sterling silver is by Christofle, France, the linens are by Frette, the crystal glasses are by Riedel, and the handcrafted Italian dinnerware is by Vietri. The Steven Volpe Design custom-made Louis XIII–style chairs are of solid walnut. The oak table is also from Volpe Design. The floor is crafted of recycled oak from a demolished house in the Napa Valley. To create the winery, Leslie Rudd worked closely with his team of full-time contractors, carpenters, and an on-site cabinetmaker.

Harvest in the Napa Valley *(left)* Rudd
Vineyards, planted to Cabernet Sauvignon,
Cabernet Franc, Malbec, Merlot, and a splash
of Petit Verdot, are situated in Oakville,
on some of the richest, reddest, and rockiest
soils in California. The volcanic rocks and
gravel, as well as the alluvial soil from the
Napa River, provide excellent drainage, an
important requirement for producing exceptional wine grapes. The 2002 Rudd Estate
Proprietary Estate wine, a blend of Cabernet
Sauvignon, Cabernet Franc, Petit Verdot,
Merlot, and Malbec, was described by
Robert M. Parker Jr. in *The Wine Advocate*
as "superb, with aromas of scorched earth,
tobacco leaf, black currants, and blueberries,
with a striking mineralogy, high tannins,
and a certain austerity, which suggest
considerable aging potential for this wine,
which is concentrated with a certain
exuberance and unctuosity but firm structure."
It was bestowed ninety-five points, out of
a possible one hundred. Leslie Rudd has
achieved his goal in his quest for excellence.

California

MODERN

—

The chief benefit of the house is that it shelters
day-dreaming. The house shelters the dreamer,
the house allows one to dream in peace.
The house is one of the greatest powers
of integration for the thoughts, memories,
and dreams of mankind.

❧

GASTON BACHELARD [1884–1962]
from *The Poetics of Space*

NAPA VALLEY MODERN

MICHAEL VANDERBYL *and* ANNA HERNANDEZ *in the Napa Valley*

———

DESIGN DEAN MICHAEL VANDERBYL AND HIS WIFE, ANNA HERNANDEZ, FOUNDER OF LUNA TEXTILES, NEVER THOUGHT THEY'D TAKE TO THE COUNTRY LIFE. THEY BOTH RUN THEIR OWN BUSINESSES IN SAN FRANCISCO AND TRAVEL OFTEN on business. They were proud urbanites, at home in big cities around the world.

More than twenty years ago, Vanderbyl founded his own multidisciplinary design firm, Vanderbyl Design, with clients that include IBM, Henredon, the San Francisco Design Center, the Walt Disney Company, and the Robert Talbott Company. Vanderbyl is also the dean of Design at California College of the Arts, his alma mater.

Hernandez is the president of Luna Textiles, an award-winning fabric design and manufacturing company with showrooms around the country. It was Hernandez, a business-minded MBA, who went property hunting in the Napa Valley and found a forlorn house on a spectacularly sited piece of land.

"The original house stood near the street, but behind it were just miles and miles of vineyards with the Mayacamas Mountains rising up in the green distance," said Vanderbyl.

"We decided to tear down the house and build a weekend bungalow using valley Craftsman cottages, wine country barns, and the agricultural vernacular for inspiration," he said.

The couple, who live, breathe, and are passionately involved in all aspects of the design world, have continued to study the history of design, interiors, and the vernacular architecture of the Napa Valley. They decided to take on this design project themselves, with the help of contractor Andrew Clyde, principal of Clyde Construction.

Rhythm of Light (opposite) The sunroom faces west toward the vineyards and the Mayacamas Mountains. The St. Helena floor lamps were designed by Michael Vanderbyl. A pair of Westwood sofas were designed by Barbara Barry. The white Spot tables are from Crate & Barrel. The graphic pattern of beams and mullions provides a dramatic frame for the 180-degree view, as well as the fifty-foot pool and shingled pool house/guesthouse. The roof trusses were inspired by the bowed truss roof of a nearby winery. The patio, with McGuire's Archetype furniture by Vanderbyl, is covered in Connecticut bluestone. Flowering cherry trees signal spring, and later lavender scents the summer night.

"Andrew's work is impeccable, and we had a like-minded attitude toward quality and craftsmanship," said Hernandez. "We all worked together well, and now we all share the pride of creating this place together."

While both Vanderbyl and Hernandez are lifelong modernists, they decided on "wine country Craftsman meets New England cottage" for their aesthetic direction. The exterior is shingled. The roof of corrugated metal is also a nod to winery architecture. Classic symmetry was their guiding principle.

"We planned the house as a place to unwind from our hectic work weeks," said Vanderbyl. "On Saturday mornings, we walk down our lane to Dean & Deluca for coffee, and on Friday mornings we shop at the St. Helena farmers' market for the freshest produce."

Anna is cultivating an English-style rose garden, with pastel Pemberton and David Austin roses. The couple spend summer days on their blissful acre working on a new wine building and reading beside the fire in winter. Nights are balmy in the Napa Valley. They swim, sit beside the pool and watch the sunset scatter pink and orange clouds across the valley, and gaze at the hills reflected in the water.

Reflections of Late Summer (*above left*) Vanderbyl and Hernandez and their friends from near and far enjoy lunches and dinners on the pool terrace from March through November. The back of the house and the pool are exposed to western light and late twilight, and the couple keeps the space uncluttered and open to vineyard views.

Spatial Play (*above right and opposite*) The couple enjoyed collaborating on every design element, including the bold corbels on the massive fireplace mantel. The Biedermeier-style chair was designed by Michael Vanderbyl for Bolier & Company. The Arthur wall sconces in the hallway are by Christian Liaigre for Holly Hunt. The hall and the main room have four-foot-six-inch wainscoting that anchors and balances the white walls. The living room is furnished with Carmel chairs and Westwood sofas by Barbara Barry covered in Emile felted wool by Luna Textiles. The St. Helena floor lamps were designed by Michael Vanderbyl.

Anna, pouring a glass of Silver Oak Cabernet Sauvignon 1993, in honor of the summer they first met, and whipping out a Tiffany box. She accepted.

They were married in a small wine country chapel and walked down the lane to their new house, led by the kilted twenty-piece Stewart Tartan Pipes and Drums in a swirl of bagpipes, and followed by two hundred guests carrying white parasols. The reception was held beside their pool, and later, as night fell, they dined beneath the stars and danced to the blues music of the Tommy Castro Band.

"In winter we watch storms come from the coast and over the Mayacamas Range," said Hernandez. "We light the fires, pour a glass or two of Cabernet, and sit in our sunroom and listen to the rain on the tin roof."

The Fourth of July is well celebrated in the valley, with small-town parades and flags flying up and down Highway 29.

"We invite lots of friends for the day and turn on all the great traditional food and Napa Valley wines," she said. "Best of all, the Mondavi winery puts on a spectacular fireworks show. We have front-row seats from our terrace, and it feels as if it's put on just for us." ✻

Saturday nights, they drive over to Press Restaurant, designed by Howard Backen, for a convivial dinner with friends. When they return, they often sit outside beside the pool for hours watching the stars, enjoying the seductive scent of ripening grapes, and listening to the country silence.

When the 2,400-square-foot house was complete and the couple had moved in, Michael proposed to

In Black and White (above) Anna Hernandez and Michael Vanderbyl are modernists at heart, but they appreciate the warmth and elegant familiarity of traditional silhouettes and grammar. The dining table, crafted by Baronian Manufacturing, and the Alder chairs, by Bernhardt, were designed by Michael Vanderbyl. The custom lighting fixture, which matches the lighting in the kitchen, is a Neidhardt lamp by Boyd Lighting, designed by Michael Vanderbyl. The Coco fabric on the dining chairs, and the chocolate wool satin textiles selected for the curtains, were both designed and crafted by Luna Textiles.

The White Album (opposite) Ten-foot pocket doors divide the dining room and the kitchen from the living room. The kitchen has a custom-crafted table, white Carrara marble countertops, and white-painted wood cabinets with crown moldings. Above the table floats a custom Neidhardt lighting fixture, designed by Michael Vanderbyl. The Emeco aluminum chairs were originally crafted for the military and served in submarines. The paint is Benjamin Moore's Navajo White. The floors are dark-stained oak. The kitchen equipment includes a Viking range, an Ann Sacks Shaw's Original sink, and a Bosch dishwasher.

THE MODERN BARN

A Healdsburg retreat designed by architects JULIE DOWLING *and* LORISSA KIMM

———

SAN FRANCISCO ARCHITECTS JULIE DOWLING AND LORISSA KIMM MET WHILE WORKING FOR ARCHITECT MICHAEL GRAVES, AFTER THEY EACH RECEIVED THEIR MASTER'S DEGREES IN ARCHITECTURE FROM PRINCETON UNIVERSITY. IN THE Graves office, they worked on five-star hotels, commercial buildings, and interiors. They moved independently to San Francisco, worked for five years with California companies, and founded Dowling Kimm Studios in 2001. The partners work on interiors and architecture projects for residences, hotels, art galleries, and a broad range of projects. Their focus is on timeless, modern design, and the architects are known for their varied palette of materials, their warm modernist architecture, and environments that are rich in natural light and texture.

Four years ago they were approached by Scott Kalmbach to design a weekend house on a hillside property near Healdsburg in the Russian River Valley. His concept was a barnlike structure with the feeling of a casual, open modern loft.

"Scott had seen my own house in Pacific Heights, in which I had inserted a modern interior into a Victorian flat," noted Dowling. He saw that we could successfully bring together traditional forms with a modern attitude.

"We drove up to look at the property and started discussing how we could successfully bring together two contrasting concepts," she said.

The two-acre site stands on a side of a wooded hill, two miles east of the town of Healdsburg. "As we walked the site, and later went through evaluation, discovery, and technical reports, we found that there was only a very small buildable area," said Dowling.

The limited space worked to their advantage, because it was in the direction of the views. The architects focused on the simplest possible shape and getting the maximum square footage.

———

California Sunshine (opposite) For their clients Scott and Tjasa Kalmbach and their children, the architects planned a simple twenty-five-hundred-square-foot structure inspired by a country barn, its lines as confident and charming as a child's drawing of a house, at once archetypal and yet entirely modern. The exterior of the house is clad in recycled old-growth redwood barn wood. Twenty-foot-tall windows wrap around the house, drawing in sunshine throughout the day.

Simple Structures *(above)* Kimm and Dowling spent months detailing and perfecting the house to make the most of its setting overlooking Healdsburg and the Russian River Valley, and to maximize summer sunshine, winter warmth, and easy access to the outdoors. The exterior is recycled old-growth redwood barn siding, with complex waterproofing and structural systems beneath.

Flirting with the Outdoors *(left and right)* In counterpoint to the barn vernacular architecture, the Kalmbachs fashioned the interiors as a mid-century modern idyll. Doors in the living room seamlessly lead outside to the pool terrace and the pool. The Kalmbachs and their friends often spend most of the day around the pool, crafting easy barbecue lunches, endlessly inventing new water sports that involve lots of splashing and nonstop laughter. The Scandinavian steel fireplace was selected for its minimalist lines and effective heating. Chaises longues beside the pool are from Design Within Reach.

The plan was to give the house all-season access to the outdoors. The weather in this wine-growing region is conducive to outdoor living year-round, and only on the January rainy days do weekenders retreat indoors.

"Our goal was to use natural materials with minimal detailing, so that the architecture and the materials would become the focus," said Dowling. "We also limited the materials within the project palette to encourage a calm and minimal environment. For us, less is more, and restraint is good."

Kimm noted that the straightforward barn/loft space and tall curtainless windows would let the outside in and create visual continuity with nature.

The program calls for a clean, rectangular foundation. A single linear pitched standing-seam roof and a repetitive fenestration allowed the architects to meet the budget and gave the house its iconic silhouette.

Kalmbach decided to clad the exterior of the barn with siding of recycled old-growth redwood barn timbers, to create a rustic appearance and to make the building one with the wooded site.

Ironically, saving the redwoods in this creative manner proved costly in this case, since the wood was uneven and had holes. The weathered siding, with areas of worn paint still visible, had great character but required the barn to be double-insulated against rain and cold weather. Yet although using reclaimed wood turned out to be expensive, it gives the barn its distinctive color and patina.

Open Door Policy *(opposite)* Dowling and Kimm planned the house with access to the terraces and decks from all sides of the house. Tall aluminum windows were crafted by Bonelli. The pedestal chairs are from West Elm. Kalmbach, Kimm, and Dowling deliberately contrasted modern classic furniture, like the glass-topped table, with the rustic, paint-chipped sideboard, soft leather pillows, and cashmere throws.

Simply Stated *(above)* The double-height entry hall and stairway create a bridge connecting the three separate bedroom suite wings on the second floor. The entry, with glass doors and tall windows, creates a transparent "slice" at the core of the house. The stairs are walnut, and the railings, custom-made, are steel.

The owners and architects decided not to overdesign the landscape. The area around the pool is planted with grasses that look native to the property. Otherwise, the land was cleared of brambles so that the children can play beneath the old oak trees. Deer often walk inquisitively up to the house and wander off to chomp grass before heading back into the woodlands.

The interior plan has a central linear axis ending in a double-height kitchen/dining room/living room, facing the pool and the view. All interior walls were painted white, with minimal detailing.

"The large and open interiors, the simplicity of the finishes, and the straightforward plan make it an extremely practical weekend house," said Dowling. "It's the kind of holiday house where you can arrive, walk in the door, put your groceries in the refrigerator, throw your bags in the bedroom, and go for a swim. There's nothing complicated. When the family leaves, they pack up and lock the gates behind them. It's a carefree house. Bringing together two classic architectural traditions—the loft and the barn—and keeping it clear and uncomplicated worked incredibly well for this family." ❧

Casual Dining and Cooking *(left and opposite)* Dowling and Kimm continued their play of design contrasts with a rustic green-painted country cabinet in the kitchen, which was custom-crafted with modernist ebonized oak cabinets. The kitchen is equipped with a Wolf range and a GE stainless-steel refrigerator. A painted sideboard provides a useful surface for a lunchtime buffet.

Light and Air *(above and right)* Incorporated in the second floor are three bedroom suites, each with bathrooms. This bedroom suite includes a sunny bedroom and a bathroom with a soaking tub, with large windows that overlook the California oaks on the property. The master suite is divided by a floating wall that serves as a tall headboard and a wall on which to hang a painting, on one side, and as a freestanding partially enclosed shower on the other. The partial wall also maintains the casual, light-filled atmosphere of the suite. The landscape painting is by Tjasa Kalmbach. Sheets are by Frette and Pratesi.

FREESTYLE COUNTRY

A weekend retreat in St. Helena for CHRISTOPHER FLACH *and* MARTHA ANGUS

———

DIVING INTO THE GREEN EMBRACE OF THE NAPA VALLEY, MARTHA ANGUS AND CHRISTOPHER FLACH HAVE CREATED A NEW HOUSE WITH ELEGANT INTERIORS FOR YEAR-ROUND LIVING. CONTEMPORARY ART AND A LIFETIME COLLECTION OF antiques are showcased in crisp, pure rooms that are as cool and comfortable as a classic white linen shirt on a hot summer day.

San Francisco interior designer Martha Angus is known for her elegant, urbane interiors and for the worldly and polished style she applies to city apartments and grand houses around the Bay Area. She founded Martha Angus, Inc., eight years ago and has become a design darling of leading art collectors.

When she and her husband, photographer Christopher Flach, built their handsome new house in the vineyards just north of St. Helena, friends and admirers were curious to see how she would translate her polished approach to country living.

"I wanted the architecture to have a timeless neo-classical feeling without the country clichés," said Angus, who worked with her colleague, building designer Phillip King Parton, on the plans. "From the first sketches and conceptual drawings and early discussions with Phillip, we worked to pare down the interiors, to keep them plain and simple, and to give the rooms a restful, serene feeling."

The house stands on a quiet country road amid noble oaks and overlooks hillsides of Merlot and Cabernet Sauvignon vines. The property is beautifully sited, with mature palm trees and aspects of eucalyptus, walnut trees, and vineyards in all directions. Acres of hillside vineyards on adjacent properties are their own borrowed landscape, without the maintenance.

The architecture took its inspiration from Andrea Palladio, who knew a thing or two about shaping classic country villas and superbly ordered interiors. The structure mimics Palladian balance, order, and rationale but rejects decorative flourishes and unnecessary visual clutter.

Playing Pool (opposite) The house overlooks hillsides of vineyards and is surrounded by mature oaks. The exterior integral-color stucco is a neutral taupe/gray tone. Landscape and pool designed by Stephen Suzman.

No one notices

Country Cycling (above) An elegant classic Hermès bicycle in the rose garden awaits a spin on country roads. The teak bench is by John Danzer for Munder Skiles. The sculpture is by Jack Youngerman.

Fire Away (left and opposite) A bolection carved French limestone fireplace with antique French firebricks gives the Rumford fireplace character and a feeling of age. A pair of custom-designed sofas are upholstered in Cowtan & Tout linen/cotton. The green blanket and apple-green cashmere throw are by Hermès. The white-enameled steel table is by Gary Hutton, through Therien Studio Workshops.

This is Martha's take on Palladio, with the classical silhouette, the perfect proportions, and a confident repetition of windows and detailing, but without the grand gestures and folderol.

Rather than adding fussy details or overtly historic references, Angus and Parton relied on classical technique like thickened walls, high ceilings, axial planning, symmetry, and simple proportions to give the modern house the classical approach they wanted.

"I wanted the house to be straightforward and airy," said Martha. "The temperature in summer often climbs up to 100 degrees, so the house has to feel light and unencumbered. There are no crown moldings, no trim, no extraneous airs and graces. We wanted the luxury of views, clear light, and a certain peace of mind that comes with unfussy interiors."

Building materials are honest and spare. The walls are stucco-tinted gray/taupe to blend in with the landscape. Floors are honed Portuguese limestone. The metal roof echoes the traditional material used on Napa Valley barns.

The interior design mixes rustic and low-key antiques with modern art. Consistent with her philosophy of keeping the background calm and plain, Martha had all walls, ceilings, and cabinetry painted in the palest gray/green/off-white custom paint by Donald Kaufman. The color, which changes from palest lichen to dove gray to chalk throughout the day, serves as a soothing counterpoint to the intense summer light in the valley.

Comfort Food (left) In the dining room, a vintage oak table with a pale blue waxed and cerused finish is spacious enough for eight friends, art projects, summer cocktails, or winter games. Around the table are gray-painted chairs by Janus et Cie.

Gray Matter (opposite) The kitchen gains its clarity and crispness from Martha's use of pale gray Donald Kaufman paint on the work island cabinetry, on walls, and on the finial-topped custom-crafted cabinet (inspired by an Italian armoire at Therien Studio Workshops) that disguises the Sub-Zero refrigerator. The pale blue Lavastone island countertop was custom ordered from Sue Fisher King. The print by Ellsworth Kelly is from the John Berggruen Gallery.

Soothing Rest *(above)* A mahogany headboard with gold Thai silk upholstery shines against the Andy Warhol silk screen. On the Thai silk sofa are silk pillows and a pink cashmere throw from Sue Fisher King. The pink python "Duchess of Windsor" telephone table is also from Sue Fisher King.

Going in Circles *(opposite)* The elliptical vestibule has a Portuguese limestone floor. A pair of French provincial chairs are juxtaposed with a series of gold-framed lithographs by Cy Twombly.

Fresh and modern, Martha's pure, cool decor and calm, beautifully edited rooms are sure to set trends in the Napa Valley for years to come.

The house is arranged around a graceful elliptical entry hall with a honed Portuguese ivory limestone floor and a central double-cube living room. Two carved pine overscale antique architectural elements from Amy Perlin Antiques in New York frame the entry into the living room.

The kitchen and dining room are open to each other. A large blue dining table is surrounded by wicker chairs from Janus et Cie.

The kitchen has no upper cabinets, allowing space for displaying art on the walls. Over the cooktop hangs a large silkscreen on paper by Ellsworth Kelly from the John Berggruen Gallery. A neoclassical armoire topped with finials, inspired by an antique armoire at Therien & Co., encloses the refrigerator. Kitchen countertops around the stove and sink are Calacatta Oro marble.

The couple worked closely with Stephen Suzman and with Colin Jones of Suzman/Cole landscape architects to place the house, with its integral-color gray stucco exterior, into the rural landscape. Mature olive trees underplanted with lavender and grasses give the house a graceful frame.

With the house complete, Flach and Angus can recall their days of searching for property with a light heart.

"We looked at Napa Valley properties for three years before we found our perfect acre," said Angus.

"We would spend weekends viewing houses up and down the valley, and even checked on the Internet, before we found this property," noted the designer.

Now the house works well both for quiet weekends and entertaining. Son Malcolm has his own suite and a media room with a vintage pinball machine. Martha and Chris have a library/study upstairs next to their quiet bedroom. And there is always the rose garden, or the vegetable garden, to draw them outside.

"We have beautiful light here all day," said Christopher. "When we arrive on Friday evenings, we pop the champagne corks and walk out into the garden. We eat tomatoes and basil straight from the garden for hors d'oeuvres. It's the best of country living." ❧

COUNTRY VIEWPOINT

Architect RICHARD BEARD *designed a modern-thinking house in*
Dry Creek Valley for BIEKE *and* BRIAN BURWELL

———

WHEN BIEKE AND BRIAN BURWELL DECIDED TO BUILD A HOUSE IN THE WINE COUNTRY NORTHWEST OF HEALDSBURG IN SONOMA COUNTY, THEY SENT ARCHITECT RICHARD BEARD A THOUGHTFUL AND INSPIRING LIST OF THEIR DREAMS, ASPIRATIONS, and requirements for the architecture. Their dramatic hillside property overlooks the Dry Creek Valley, a top wine appellation with twenty-five wineries and more than six thousand acres planted to grapes. World-class Zinfandel, Sauvignon Blanc, Merlot, and Chenin Blanc wines are grown in this region, about one hour's drive north of San Francisco.

"My clients said that they wanted a house that would be easy to maintain, that they expected a lot of visitors, and that they intended to fill the house with friends, as well as their three sons and eventually their families," noted Beard, a founder of BAR Architects, a ten-year-old firm based in San Francisco. "Their wish list included a big family gathering room, a smaller, more intimate room for Bieke and Brian, and rooms that were versatile, comfortable, and hospitable in summer and winter."

In their manifesto, the Burwells asked for understated rooms and a Zen-like residence that was at one with the landscape. They also requested architecture with a classical feeling, and some organic touches. The house should have a strong sense of informality and relaxation, and provoke a true feeling of country, they said, without falling into the country French style or Tuscan traditional architecture traps.

The Burwells' brief: "Make the house simple but still architecturally challenging. Take an understated approach to materials, and keep the architecture sophisticated but not showy. Design it to be naturally warm in winter and cool in summer. We both hate air-conditioning. We like rooms that feel airy and open during the day and romantic at night."

Hours Pass in Peace (opposite) Weathered cedar chairs, their blocky shapes inspired by Donald Judd's sculptural art, offer comfortable viewpoints from the terrace outside the living and dining room. Beyond sheltering trees are a wild valley and natural forest. The walls of the house are concrete, stucco, and cedar. Landscape design is by Bill Bauer and James David, of Gardens, in Austin, Texas.

The couple—Bieke, an arts enthusiast, is originally from Belgium, and Brian, a partner with Marakon Associates, a management-consulting firm, grew up in Sonoma County—also imagined a house that revealed itself slowly as the family and guests headed up the hillside driveway.

"We wanted a house that shows a good understanding and use of seasonal sunshine and takes advantage of the wind blowing through the canyon without our having to deal with drafts or slamming doors. We did not want the house subjected to afternoon sun so strong we would have to live with shades closed most of the time," said Bieke, who collects contemporary California art. "We thought it would be nice to have some sun in the morning while drinking coffee, and during the day throughout most of the winter."

There was one more consideration in their highly detailed outline.

"We would prefer that the outdoor areas overlook the vineyards and the canyon, and that they should be somewhat elevated," wrote the Burwells. "We don't want to worry about snakes."

The couple's list was precise, and their ability to communicate both specific requirements and philosophical points got the project off to a fine start. They became Beard's dream clients.

"When I first visited the site, I was impressed by the beauty of the location and the uniqueness of the setting above a valley of vineyards, but I also knew that siting the house would be a challenge," said Beard. "After walking the site extensively, I could see that there was no flat land. There's a creek bordering one side of the property, with potential for flooding in winter. Several parts of the hillside were landslide prone."

Eventually, the architect sited the house on a plateau midway up the property, with views to the canyon on the south side, and to the open expanse of the valley on the north. It was easily accessible for a driveway and parking.

"Once we'd figured out the basic placement, I took into consideration that they were enthusiastic and informed antiques and art connoisseurs, and that their expanding collections would have to be accommodated," said Beard. "My clients are wonderful hosts, and not overly formal. I'd visited them when they were living in London and had observed how they entertain and live. Their notes and my understanding of their lifestyle informed the whole design."

The climate that is so conducive to grape growing offers extended periods of heat from June through fall harvest, along with weeks of foggy, misty, cold days in winter when the vines are dormant.

Confidently Cool (opposite) The living room walls are ivory-pale hand-crafted veneer plaster, and the floor is a hand-finished and waxed concrete. French doors open to a large shaded terrace overlooking a wild canyon with manzanita, madrone, and redwood trees. A stone-topped table designed by Belgian *antiquaire* Axel Vervoordt stands in front of a traditional English sofa with down-filled cushions. Interior design is by Michael Booth, Babey Moulton Jue & Booth, San Francisco.

"We planned the house for both very warm summer days, and for cool rainy weather," said the architect.

Cedar and steel awnings shade the windows and French doors from sun on hot days and allow sunshine to flood the house during winter.

Materials selected included Western red cedar and concrete for the exterior. Interior walls are ivory-colored Venetian plaster, which has a rich, soft glow, along with American cherry floors, which were hand scraped to give them a richer, more country-friendly texture.

"The floor feels great beneath bare feet," noted Beard. It's a very indoor/outdoor house. Terraces are as important to the daily rhythms as enclosed interiors. Each room is matched with an expansive and very accessible loggia or a large courtyard.

It was planned from the first meetings to be a very understated place, never designed to impress or over-whelm visitors. The architecture is superbly delineated, a backdrop to the bounty of hills, forest, and valley.

The luxury is in the setting, in the controlled and intentional simplicity of the architecture, and in the way the design embraces and enhances the views and open air. The architect and landscape designers worked conscientiously to save trees on the property, both for reasons of ecology and to provide natural shade for the terraces and courtyards surrounding the house.

"My clients often tell me that they reread the original list of requirements for the architecture, and they check off every point," noted Beard. "One lesson we learned is that they wanted a simple house, and it is a lot of work to keep a design uncomplicated. We accomplished everything they dreamed of. They say they feel very happy and inspired in the house. They enjoy it every day. I could not be more pleased." ❧

The Art of Ideas (above) The dining room is situated at one side of the living room and is accessible to the kitchen and the open terrace. The pale-gray waxed concrete floor is a perfect foil for the bold lines of the dining table by San Francisco sculptor Peter Gutkin. An antique Asian table from Axel Vervoordt and a revolving display of sculpture and paintings give the entry poise and character. The stairway rises to a study and then to the master bedroom.

Farmers' Market Feasting (opposite) Brian and Bieke Burwell asked architect Richard Beard to design a versatile kitchen. It's a practical room, with handmade ceramic tiles on the wall behind the stove, a work island crafted of cherry, and large windows. Countertops are honed Colacata marble.

ESSENCE OF SIMPLICITY

LEE VON HASSELN's Pebble Beach house was designed and built with Earth-friendly ideals

————

ART COLLECTOR LEE VON HASSELN'S NEW RESIDENCE STANDS PERFECTLY POISED AMONG CENTURY-OLD COASTAL OAK TREES, REDWOODS, CYPRESS, AND SYCAMORES. ITS SUPERB CUBISTIC DESIGN, DESIGNED AND PLANNED BY VON HASSELN, was inspired by the philosophy and award-winning designs of Mexican architect Luis Barragán and his disciple architect Ricardo Legorreta. Like Barragán, von Hasseln followed traditional Mission-style architecture and circled the house around a courtyard and the garden. Also like Barragán, who pared down interiors to essential geometries, she shaped a series of simply detailed rooms that have a powerful sense of meditative beauty.

"I felt from the beginning that this house and the landscape should be built with ecological principles in mind," said von Hasseln. "I wanted this to be a thoughtful house. I taught myself everything about energy conservation and passive solar heat collection. At the same time, I planned a house that would sit elegantly on the land and that would be as pared down and aesthetically balanced as Philip Johnson's famous glass house."

Her house has created a buzz in the architecture and garden communities around the world and has become a magnet for English landscape designers and New York architects. The newest concepts of ecology and conservation sit comfortably with elegant architecture and classic interiors. The new 2,400-square-foot house in Pebble Beach proves that earth-friendly design plans, solar power generation, and a garden designed for water conservation can also be very stylish, luxurious, and modern.

Equally important, the garden conserves water with 252 native trees that depend only on rainfall and benefits from a series of rainwater-collection urns. The house has no lawn requiring mowers, chemicals, or leaf blowers.

Roof-mounted solar photovoltaic collectors generate energy so efficiently that the house turns energy back into the grid, and von Hasseln has no power bills. The house is primarily heated by sunshine on the limestone floors with added insulation to retain warmth.

Into the Light (opposite) Clear glass walls that soar nine and a half feet high open the south-facing house to views of the garden and century-old oak trees around the perimeter of the two-acre property. A two-foot overhang shades the living room and study from afternoon sun.

The Contrast of Old and New *(above)* An eighteenth-century Queen Anne walnut highboy and a pair of Hepplewhite chairs with Thai silk cushions give a sense of texture and history to the sunny living room, which overlooks a garden planted with irises, tulips, daffodils, and anemones. Portraits and paintings are by von Hasseln's former husband, Lloyd Strathearn.

Simple Elegance *(opposite)* A Georgian wing chair upholstered in French linen adds its curves and sculpture to the lighthearted living room. The footstool with cabriole legs is eighteenth-century Dutch rococo. A pair of paintings is by Taos-based Russian Impressionist Nicolai Fechin, from the early twentieth century. The handcrafted Tibetan carpet was designed to be harmonious with the French limestone floor.

Lee von Hasseln is a fine arts graduate, a knowledgeable landscape designer, and a student of architecture, so she applied herself enthusiastically to the design of her new residence in Pebble Beach.

"I knew exactly what I wanted, so I drew up my own plans, made scale models, and worked out the floor plan," said von Hasseln, who grew up in Southern California and moved to Pebble Beach in 1960. Her scale models were presented to oversight committees and planning groups, along with the floor plans and blueprints. She worked out all construction details of the house with a structural engineer. Gerald Heisel, a Carmel general contractor, helped her to realize her dream.

"I wanted the house to be very open," she said. "I live alone, so I designed it strictly for myself. I could make this an 'unprivate' house, with a series of open rooms leading off the central broad hallway."

The two-acre property, part of the former Griffin estate, faces south, which made it the ideal site for her sun-fueled house.

"I studied the work of Barragán and Legorreta and gained insight into their beautiful courtyard houses," she noted. The pared-down simple cubistic shapes of the exterior, and the straightforward floor plan were also Barragán inspired.

"I studied modern lofts to make the most of the openness of these rooms," said von Hasseln.

Honed limestone floors throughout the house also make this a very low-maintenance house (von Hasseln lives with two black Labradors, Joaquin and Annie). There is radiant heat in the floors, if needed, from a low-energy boiler.

Garden Fresh (left) Dutch irises are arranged in an antique cut-glass vase from Guadalajara on a McGuire table. The blue-and-white bowls are Japanese.

Ancient and Modern (opposite) In the study, a handsome late-seventeenth-century William and Mary oyster veneer chest of drawers is juxtaposed with a modern steel desk crafted by Jim Wood, a Carmel Valley sculptor. The occasional chair is an early American Queen Anne, circa 1740.

"I generate all my own electricity and heating from the solar collectors on the roof," said von Hasseln. "Since I feed energy back to the grid, I generate electricity for others in the community."

Glass-window walls that stand nine and a half feet were crafted from three-quarter-inch-thick tempered glass laminated with ultraviolet film, to comply with energy codes, for energy efficiency and to prevent sun damage. The glass panels, which fit into stainless steel channels in the floor and ceiling, were crane-lifted into place. They are mitered at the corners. Doors to the garden are glass, with stainless-steel handles.

With richly textured cream-colored Venetian plaster walls as background, rooms are decorated with a fine international collection of rare antiques collected by

von Hasseln over the last five decades, as well as dramatic Russian Impressionist portraits and landscapes and seascapes by Nicolai Fechin (1881–1955) and Leon Gaspard (1882–1964).

Antiques include a stately late-seventeenth-century William and Mary oyster veneer chest of drawers, an eighteenth-century Queen Anne walnut highboy, and a pair of mid-eighteenth-century Dutch rococo footstools.

Von Hasseln planned the rooms to be uncluttered and simple, so the beautifully crafted antiques are all shown to full advantage against the neutral colors of walls and the floor. Even the bedroom has no curtains. A folding screen of birch and etched Lucite afford privacy and light control.

On moonlit nights, the glass-window walls seem to disappear, and the garden's white flowers and oak trees are clearly visible, illuminated in the bright silvery light.

"I love the openness of the house, and I use every room, every corner," said von Hasseln. "I have enjoyed the interiors even more than I expected. It fits my life so well. I would not change a thing." ✖

Sweet Repose (opposite) In the bedroom, which overlooks the garden, is a brushed steel four-poster bed custom-crafted by David Marasco in the Carmel Valley. The antique table, left, is Queen Anne. A custom-crafted birch shoji screen adds a sense of privacy.

Private Collection (left) On a shelf in the hallway, late-eighteenth-century Wedgwood bisque game dishes are arranged beside Japanese blue-and-white jars and a hand-painted bowl.

California

GARDENS

———

*La nature au lit se repose, Mars descend au jardin désert et lace
les boutons de rose dans leur corset de velours vert.*

While nature sleeps in her bed, March descends to the deserted
garden and laces rosebuds into their bodices of green velvet.

❧

Théophile Gautier [1811–1872]
from *"Premier Sourire du Printemps"*
("The First Smile of Spring"),
Émaux et Camées

CULTIVATING BEAUTY

KAYE *and* RICHARD HEAFEY'*s*
weekend house and clematis farm in Chalk Hill, Sonoma County

———

MORE THAN A DOZEN YEARS AGO, BAY AREA DESIGNER KAYE HEAFEY DINED AT CHEZ PANISSE IN BERKELEY AND HAD A EUREKA MOMENT. WILD TANGLES OF CLEMATIS WERE ARRANGED IN AN ANTIQUE BRONZE URN. HEAFEY LOVED THE BAROQUE TWISTS OF THE vines and the deep purple and blue star-shaped blooms. Kaye Heafey was so inspired by the intense colors of the clematis and the romantic and graceful tendrils of the vines that she headed for her favorite florist to buy some to arrange at home. She quickly discovered that clematis were not commercially grown. The flowers were thought to be too fragile.

Heafey believed that there was a market for cut clematis and decided to grow the elegant flowers at the 120-acre Sonoma County property she owns with her husband, Richard, a professor of ethics at the University of San Francisco.

Chalk Hill Clematis, with fifteen acres of clematis under cultivation, is now the largest grower of premium field-grown clematis in the world. The Heafeys and their farm manager, Murray Rosen, have also become experts on the cultivation of clematis plants, offering three hundred varieties for sale from their nursery near Healdsburg.

They recently opened a half-acre display garden, designed by Dublin, Ireland-based Dr. Mary Toomey, author of *The Encyclopedia of Clematis*. The garden demonstrates the myriad ways that clematis can be combined in the garden with roses, trees, and shrubs. "Officially, our business is called Ornamental Agriculture, which makes it sound so much easier than it is," Heafey said. "We had no mentors, no business model, so we had to struggle. Today nothing is treated with more dignity and luxury than those plants. Our goal is to create perfection and rare beauty."

The Joy of Summer (opposite) Kaye and Richard Heafey's Healdsburg terrace feels as if it has levitated among the leafy branches of old oak and manzanita trees. Teak chaises longues and tables invite guests to stay and enjoy the silence, the dappled sunlight, and the warm summer air. Kaye Heafey brings clematis from the barn and arranges the vines in terra-cotta urns, white-painted iron urns, and glass vases. Among her favorites is the pristine white Marie Boisselot with a pale creamy center. "On weekends, we're likely to be hosting visits from passionate clematarians and rosarians," she said.

Along the way, the Heafeys have also renovated the ranch house that was on their property, remodeling it into an airy, chic, and comfortable weekend retreat. Kaye Heafey fills the rooms with clematis and roses.

Among the cut flowers and plants offered by Chalk Hill Clematis are some of the most exquisite classic clematis. Varieties include Daniel Deronda, with large flowers in purple-blue tones with feathery pale cream anthers; Chalcedony, a pale green-white full double; Durandii, with bell-shaped blue-purple flowers; and Étoile de Paris, a delicate azure.

Kaye Heafey and Murray Rosen have edited and selected all the plants in the nursery, and Heafey's favorites include Henryi, with very elegant, pristine

white flowers; Mrs. Cholmondeley, with blooms in palest blue-mauve; Viticella Étoile Violette, star-shaped flowers in rich purple; and General Sikorski, a classic in variegated mauve-purple with intense color and rounded tepals. (Clematis have tepals, not sepals, and no petals.)

The clematis farm operation was initially pure experimentation, all trial and error, said Kaye Heafey. Each summer, she and Rosen went on wild chases around the grand gardens of Europe, poking their noses into obscure clematis nurseries all over England in search of rare and unusual plants, meeting obsessive and unknown hybridizers along the way.

"We visited all the unsung heroes of the clematis world and discovered eccentric and out-of-the-way growers," said Heafey. "We trudged through rain and mud up to our ankles but would find forty or more new hybrids to add to our list."

"For the cut-flower market, we have selected large-flowered clematis, and we have figured out ways of growing them and cutting them so that they have a beautiful character, ship well, and still retain their graceful form that bends and twists," said Heafey. "The foliage of each stem varies, in color and silhouette. They look natural—not that cookie-cutter hothouse look."

Flower Power (*above and opposite*) Kaye Heafey uses the limestone dining table as a stage for bravura displays of cut flowers and branches from the Chalk Hill Clematis nursery. Her summer floral celebration often includes arching canes of Bobby James as well as deep, dark violet Petite Faucon clematis, Ville de Lyon roses, and Durandii, a saturated dark-blue clematis with a vibrant yellow center. The hardy clematis are grown naturally on fifteen acres of shaded fields. Kaye Heafey worked with San Francisco interior designer Richard Cardello on the decor of the house. A four-door eighteenth-century French walnut armoire is used for linen and silver storage. The custom dining table was designed by Richard Cardello Interior Design. The hand-painted silk lantern is by Feneri through Sloan Miyasato, San Francisco.

The farm now ships premium cut flowers to flower markets in New York, Los Angeles, St. Louis, San Francisco, and Denver. Top flower stylists have sent the blooms to longtime clients like Sting, himself a noted gardener, Annette de la Renta, and Bette Midler.

"If a variety is too blowsy or aggressively striped or comes in a vulgar or psychedelic color, we don't grow it," Heafey said. "If it turns out to be too fragile or skimpy, I yank it out. I'm ruthless."

Clematis can look modern and classic or baroque, said Patric Powell, a San Francisco floral designer who recently celebrated his thirtieth year in business. He likes to use them for wedding decor. Chalk Hill Clematis vines bloom from April to October.

Heafey and Rosen have succeeded not only in growing healthy, sturdy plants, but also in carefully editing selections of hues. The colors of the flowers cultivated at the nursery range from icy white and cream to celadon, pale lavender, mauve, cerulean, pink, deep purple, midnight blue, azure, claret, and periwinkle blue.

Blue is rare in nature, so the blue or purple clematis can be an elegant counterpoint to pink or white roses.

"In a garden, clematis are an ideal companion to roses, and they love to climb trees and ramble over arches," Rosen said. "If you grow roses successfully, you can easily grow clematis."

Propagated in appropriate conditions, clematis require very little care. Chalk Hill Clematis are raised organically—with no pesticides and all organic fertilizers.

Rosen said their strong plants are usually immune to bugs and aphids. Clematis thrive in hundred-degree days and can survive late frosts

"Murray is an artist, and he has brought his sense of artfulness and beauty to Chalk Hill Clematis," said Kaye Heafey. "This has been the most joyful and satisfying project. I adore all the clematis. My current favorite is Louise Rowe, an exquisite lavender color, but we're always planting new varieties, and I fall in love with all of them." ❧

Deserved Repose (opposite) The massive four-poster bed is draped with a Larsen embroidered textile from India, in natural and taupe. A pair of eighteenth-century French painted commodes, restored by Sen's Antiques, are used as nightstands, with Italian Paralume glass table lamps from Policelli. Interior design by Richard Cardello.

Contemplating Nature (above) Kaye Heafey and her farm manager have spent more than a dozen years cultivating clematis. Through floods in their first season, chilly winters, heat waves, as well as calm and balmy seasons, they have trained clematis to grow gracefully and with longer stems that make arranging easy.

GOLDEN DAYS

MARIA MANETTI FARROW *cultivates roses in the heart of Napa Valley*

———

WHEN MARIA MANETTI FARROW ACQUIRED HER FIFTEEN-ACRE RUTHERFORD ESTATE FIFTEEN YEARS AGO, SHE COULD HARDLY HAVE IMAGINED THAT ONE DAY SHE WOULD WIN AWARDS FOR HER ORGANIC OLIVE OILS, DRAW PRAISE FOR HER WINES, DAZZLE gifted musicians, and delight her friends with the grapes, vegetables, fruit, and exquisite wines from her own soil.

"I've made the enhancement of life my career," said the vivacious Farrow, who grew up in Florence and came to the United States in 1976. "I love life, I love growing things, I adore gardening, and I love people. My passions come together here at Villa Mille Rose."

For the past decade, Farrow has spent her energy and creativity nurturing her vineyards, planting olive trees to make fine Tuscan-style extra-virgin olive oil, and producing her own balsamic vinegar in a Napa Valley *acetaia*.

She is also a generous patron of music and opera groups in the Napa Valley, and a longtime supporter of the San Francisco Opera and San Francisco Symphony, along with other cultural organizations around the world.

"Producing quality things from the earth gives me great pleasure, especially when I can share them with my friends," said Farrow. Weekend visitors return to the city laden with baskets of wine, olive oil, tomatoes, pomegranates, apricots, white peaches, pears, lettuces, herbs, walnuts, roses, and persimmons.

During the summer, her entertaining schedule revs up to include Saturday lunches and Sunday brunches in the garden, as well as formal dinners for friends and visiting musicians.

"The art of dining, selecting the best wines, and giving my friends enjoyment are the greatest pleasures of my life," said the glamorous Farrow, who also keeps residences in San Francisco and Florence.

A Rose by Any Other Name (opposite) Maria Manetti Farrow called her Napa Valley residence Villa Mille Rose, the "villa of a thousand roses." She has many more than a thousand. Roses spill down trellises on the exterior walls of her house and clamber over and along wooden fences that surround her rose garden; carefully trained standard roses like Brandy stand tall around the perimeter of her swimming pool and lawns. One of her favorites is Coral Dawn, which blooms all summer and is hardy throughout the seasons in Napa Valley. From her windows and terrace, Farrow views her own vineyards and a romantic landscape of cypresses, olive orchards, oleanders, irises, box hedges, and centuries-old native oak trees. The cypresses and roses remind Farrow of her native Florence.

From her handsome Tuscany-inspired villa, she can see verdant landscapes, rustic old oaks, and forty-two acres of her vineyards planted to Chardonnay, Cabernet Sauvignon, and Merlot.

In the culinary garden are rows of fava beans, fifteen kinds of salad greens, herbs, five kinds of beets, and artichokes, asparagus, and tomatoes. Beyond the swimming pool and allées of pink and white oleanders and forsythias is a fruit orchard of white peaches, nectarines, Santa Rosa plums, apricots, melons, heirloom apples, and Japanese pears.

"Even when I'm superexhausted from a long trip, I get an injection of energy as soon as I arrive here in the Napa Valley," said Farrow, who recently traveled to Florence and Parma to study Italy's historic architecture

and to London, St. Petersburg, and New York to support the cities' symphony orchestras.

Maria Manetti Farrow first made her mark in the seventies and eighties distributing Gucci, Fendi, and Mark Cross accessories in the United States and Canada.

"I loved being a business executive, and after I sold the business in 1989 I had a few doubts about a new direction," said Farrow. "I've poured my energy into Villa Mille Rose, shaping my garden. Producing quality products from the earth has become an intensely interesting business. In the wine industry, there is always drama and pleasure, equally."

She moved to the Napa Valley because it reminded her of her beloved Chianti Classico, forty-five minutes from Florence, where she had a villa with gardens, vegetables, and olive trees.

"Every season here is fulfilling," she said, clipping roses to arrange in her living room. "The Napa Valley is one of the most beautiful regions in the world. I am so lucky, so grateful, to be living here. My roses are flourishing, the irises have a brief and beautiful season, and in the valley, every season is beautiful." ❧

Let a Thousand Roses Bloom (opposite and above) Farrow, who also produces her own wine under her Villa Mille Rose label, has spent more than a decade working on her rose garden. Around the perimeter she has placed traditional Italian stone statuary like the dolphins at left, to lend the enclosed garden structure and variation. An enthusiastic rose grower, Farrow does not focus on one color or type of rose, but demands that they produce all summer and that their stems and buds look as beautiful in a vase as they do in the garden.

Ruffles and Flourishes *(opposite and above)* Maria Manetti Farrow admires the traditional Italian combination of irises and roses and has planted irises, including the blue bearded iris, Germanic hybrid, en masse, creating a sea of blue and green. The bold scale of the irises, which flourish in the Napa Valley, and the gray-green color and scythelike shape of the leaves make a graphic contrast with her carefully clipped rose bushes. On the exterior walls of her Rutherford house, food and wine grower and entrepreneur Farrow trained Coral Dawn on trellises. The rose has thrived in a Napa Valley microclimate that includes cool, foggy winters and hot, dry summers.

PEACE AND PERFECTION

BRUNNO *and* URANNIA RISTOW *cultivate their gardens*
and vineyard high above the Napa Valley

———

"I'M ALWAYS OVERWHELMED BY THE BEAUTY OF THE NAPA VALLEY," SAID BRUNNO RISTOW, AN INTERNATIONALLY FAMOUS PLASTIC SURGEON WITH A PRIVATE CLINIC IN SAN FRANCISCO. "IT'S BEAUTIFUL YEAR-ROUND. WHEN WE ARRIVE THERE on Friday nights, the air is scented with ripening grapes, roses, rosemary, and ancient oaks. In winter when the vines are bare, the valley air is fresh and clear."

Dr. Ristow and his wife, Urannia, acquired their property, which is a one-hour drive north of San Francisco, more than twenty-three years ago.

"We called the place Quinta de Pedras, which is Portuguese for 'estate of stones,'" noted Brunno.

Creating and nurturing extraordinarily lavish gardens and vineyards on their rock-strewn hill to the east of the Silverado Trail became their passion.

"This has been our horticultural education, as well as a deeply satisfying project," said Urannia, who designed and planned the flower gardens. "The terraces, pathways, and vineyard were all excavated with heavy earth-moving equipment to build a formal structure. We had to create a healthy soil level for vineyards, as well as for the maples, yews, and cypress."

Their weekend retreat was a rock-clearing geology project for several years before it became a place of repose. Every rose bush and every vine became the subject of trial and error.

Ristow Estate grapes are grown exclusively in the Quinta de Pedras Vineyard located on the Silverado Trail, just south of the Stags Leap appellation. The eighteen-acre vineyard lies on a south-facing hillside and is planted solely to Cabernet Sauvignon.

———

Music Fills the Air (opposite) Brunno and Urannia Ristow, working with designer Richard Tam, planned the living room for entertaining groups of friends. The house is a place of reflection and creativity when they escape to the country on weekends. Ceilings are high, so they selected large-scale furniture, including a Louis XVI-style table, a marble pedestal table, and a grand piano. The room's French doors lead to the swimming pool on the west side and to the garden and duck pond on the north. Dinner guests gather in the living room, walking out onto the terrace where an orchestra plays. Architecture is by Sandy Walker, Walker & Moody, San Francisco.

Brunno was persuaded to grow grapes after neighboring vintner Gene Trefethen extolled the virtues of south-facing hillsides and rocky terrain as a classic combination for growing outstanding Cabernet Sauvignon with great character.

The original vine roots hit bedrock, so a portion of the first vineyard was eventually replanted with new clones that were more appropriate for the rocky terrain, and the new vines now bear delicious and intense fruit. The soil and the terrain impart a distinctive minerality

to the fruit and lend spice flavors characteristic of each Ristow Estate Cabernet Sauvignon vintage. The Ristow Estate label produces a thousand cases each year.

Wine Spectator has written that the "Ristow Estate Cabernet blend consistently delivers outstanding intensity and balance," and Ristow Estate Cabernet Sauvignon vintages have been described as an idyllic marriage of fruit and oak and the desirable but elusive quality the French call *terroir*.

The Ristow family, now weekend farmers, continue to experiment and to work on their garden. Holidays there are endless lunches on the terrace. Urannia plants more roses and supervises olive harvests. Brunno excavated a pond with an island to encourage migrating geese.

"I brought in canvasbacks, and pintails, and blackneck swans for their beauty and character," said Brunno. "In season, Canadian geese gather in the evening, and our pond becomes the Ristow Diner. I feed them all cracked corn enhanced with vitamins to keep them and their young healthy. Our property is a retreat for us, and it's also become a haven for the birds. Birds nest in the trees. Now our garden is a sanctuary for wildlife. Our life has been so enriched by this beautiful place." ❧

Flora and Fantasy (opposite) On the Ristows' hillside, a group of graceful white and pink dogwoods have been planted in harmony with pink and white azaleas. They're sheltered beneath the canopy of old oak trees, which protect the delicate spring blossoms from occasional icy gusts.

Signs of Early Spring (left) Vigorous white wisteria has been trained to grow on a loggia column near the swimming pool. Wisteria flourishes in the Napa Valley and is usually in full bloom in April and May.

Italian Renaissance (right and above) White and blue iris, French lavender, and varieties of climbing roses grow around the perimeter of the duck pond. An antique Italian stone urn provides an elegant perch for ivy.

Graceful Garlands (far right) White wisteria, now well established, has been trained to grow in long trailing garlands on the fences surrounding the tennis courts. Wisteria is usually in full romantic bloom early in spring, before roses come into bud. It leafs out for the summer, and after leaves fall in November, the knots and twists of vines create graphic sculptures.

Napa Valley View *(left and above)* Boxwood hedges, ivy swags, and Brandy roses border the lawn surrounding the pool. Globes of boxwood are planted in Italian stone urns. The Ristows can watch their Ristow Estate Cabernet Sauvignon vineyards flourishing, with the Napa Valley and the San Pablo Bay in the distance. They were inspired by swimming pools they had seen in Mexico and in Hawaii to commission students at Napa Valley College to create a large floral motif, crafted in tiles.

Creating Garden Structure *(pages 130–131)* The garden is landscaped with a loggia and stone walls crafted out of field stones removed from the vineyards. "With gardens and vineyards, it's a process of planting, experimenting, and designing—and hoping. The seasons are exciting and often surprising," said Urannia Ristow. "We planted an orange grove and lost it all in an unusually hard frost. We planted poplars and wisteria, which have flourished." The family's gardeners tried roses, including Peace, Mr. Lincoln, and Queen Elizabeth, and they have all so done well that the Ristows have planted more than two hundred rose varieties. "We began with five acres, and we now have twenty-seven," said Brunno. "On the hillside are the vineyard, fig, apple, lemon, plum, and pear trees. Every October we harvest olives and press extra-virgin olive oil. Being part of the rhythms of the seasons and of nature is extremely fulfilling."

California

SPIRIT

———

*Une jolie habitation ne rend-elle pas l'hiver
plus poétique, et l'hiver n'augment-t-il
la poésie de l'habitation?*

Isn't it true that a pleasant house makes
winter more poetic, and doesn't winter add
to the poetry of a house?

❧

CHARLES BAUDELAIRE [1821–1867]
from *Les Paradis Artificiels*

INTO THE WOODS

PAUL WISEMAN *and* RICHARD SNYDER's *weekend retreat in Mill Valley*

———

DURING THE WEEK, ATTORNEY (AND HISTORIAN AND SCIENTIST MANQUÉ) RICHARD NEIL SNYDER AND HIS PARTNER, INTERIOR DESIGNER PAUL VINCENT WISEMAN, LIVE AT THEIR HISTORIC VILLA ON THE HIGHEST POINT OF BELVEDERE, A FABLED peninsula across the bay from San Francisco. On weekends, they head for their country retreat in Mill Valley, just twenty minutes from Belvedere but worlds away in style and aspect.

While the extroverted Belvedere villa opens to bay views, salty breezes, and early-morning sunshine, their Mill Valley cottage is introverted and enclosed, surrounded by second-growth redwoods, and dappled and romantically shaded.

Snyder acquired their retreat in 1974.

It was originally built as a summerhouse in 1886 for the Newbegin family, who were noted booksellers in San Francisco since the days of the Gold Rush. It was originally called Earnscliff, since it stands above Earnscliff Creek, which eventually runs into Mill Creek in the center of Mill Valley.

It's a balloon construction of heart of redwood, so it survived the 1906 earthquake undamaged, and the framing is termite free.

"The house had been aggressively remodeled in the fifties, so the renovation included updating, repair, and restoration of every inch, from the foundation upward," he said.

They used as their guideline the original Craftsman-Mission style, adding redwood shingles to the exterior.

"We took four years to make it a ground-up, truly historic renovation, so that it will last another hundred years," said Snyder. "We added new traditional-style bathrooms, a new terrace, a new skylight in the study/dining room, and built-in bookshelves in every room except the bathroom and the kitchen."

Hope Springs Supernal (opposite) The Mill Valley retreat is surrounded by California bay trees, madrones, and redwoods. In spring and summer, Snyder and Wiseman can take breakfast on the bluestone terrace, lingering over the *New York Times* and taking in the silence. The Costa Rican teak chairs and tables were designed by their friend John Danzer for Munder Skiles. The lantern is a Japanese antique. Every window of the house opens onto a green curtain of superbly maintained trees, the arborist's art. Richard Snyder calls their redwood-shaded enclave "a residential Muir Woods."

Snyder, an avid bibliophile and a lifelong collector of minerals, has amassed an idiosyncratic library, which includes incunabula from the fifteenth century, as well as contemporary signed first editions. He has mineral collections of rare Mesozoic fossils from California, meteorites, and fluorescent specimens; rare pyrrhotites and tourmalines from Tsumeb, Namibia; as well as a complete lanthanide series of available mineral specimens, all displayed museum-style in locked and secured cabinets.

"The living room is the most authentic of all the rooms," noted Wiseman. "We built in window seats, installed slightly larger windows, and put in new hardwood floors, but the ceiling beams and interior architecture are the originals."

Every corner of the room is crammed (well, beautifully styled) with collections of paintings, musical instruments, tortoiseshell objects, and books that have now spilled out of the secretary, the shelf, and the tables.

The Designer's Eye (opposite) With its new peaked skylight, the study also serves occasionally as a dining room. For their pleasure the owners have assembled on an oak table beautiful objects, including a solitaire board game of mineral spheres, designed by Snyder. Wiseman grew up on a pear farm in the California Delta and now collects pear-wood tea caddies and other pear memorabilia.

The Connoisseur's Library (top right) A Chinese Warring States pre-Han urn dynasty stands on a Victorian plinth in the study. Plaster body casts, found in an antique store in London, were crafted in the twenties by a Belgian artist. They are blackened from a long-ago conflagration in Belgium. Snyder has been collecting rare and specialized books since he was a boy, and his collection now numbers into the thousands. The walls and woodwork were painted white, with an antique glaze developed by Elisa Stancil to make them look older.

Green, Green, It's Green They Say (bottom right) Towering, noble redwoods, surround the house. Mill Valley is a mere twenty-minute drive from downtown San Francisco, but feels far removed from city cares.

Calm and Collected *(left and above right)* Dramatic ceiling beams, original to the house, crisscross the living room as a counterpoint to the Roman antiquities and highly detailed antiques and vivid collections. A pair of painted Italian benches, found in London, were upholstered in white linen to serve as a plinth for a Roman bronze, and books. An English secretary, from 1810, holds Wiseman's signed first editions by Bloomsbury writers. Next to it stands an English Regency portfolio cabinet, which holds paintings, engravings, and drawings. The musical instruments include an Amati violin, a 1920s ukulele, a Ramirez Spanish guitar, and a German recorder, all part of Snyder's collection.

Not Exactly Minimalist *(above left)* On the wall is a portrait of Charles II, by the school of Sir Peter Lely, the fashionable Dutch-born painter. A collection of antique tortoiseshell tea caddies, musical instruments, card cases, and boxes dated from the late eighteenth century to the early nineteenth century stands on a nineteenth-century Dutch copy of an English Queen Anne table.

Snyder's books include sets of historical atlases from 1754 to the present, a complete set of Albert Skira art books, the complete Bollingen Series on the scientific works of Jung, and an incunabulum of Suetonius XII Caesurum, 1484, along with Lovecraft, Sackville-West, Robert W. Chambers, and books on aesthetics and architecture.

The books are carefully curated by subject, but the overflow has now crept onto the floor, where stacks rise like ziggurats, even in the living room, where Snyder also keeps his collections of musical scores.

Wiseman's antique tortoiseshell tea caddies and musical instrument collection stand on a Dutch copy of an English table.

"It's one of those 'off' pieces that I love," noted Wiseman. The table is a contrivance, a charming combination of oddly shaped legs and a chinoiserie-painted top in a Netherlandish interpretation of the Chinese style.

"The changes of seasons are subtle here," said Snyder. "When we arrive on a rainy night in winter, the house is very welcoming. We are aware of the sun's progress, from the brief midday light in winter, to the intense dappled rays of summer. The trees keep the house warm in winter and cool in summer. Our books, the mineral collections, and our other collections enhance the sense of a retreat for study and contemplation."

Wiseman said that though they may plan to watch classic black-and-white films on DVD, they become distracted by nature's drama.

"When the wind blows, the trunks of the old redwoods move, and it is like being on a ship," said the designer. "Rain dripping down and drenching the trees is mesmerizing. When we leave on Monday morning to start the work week, we are truly inspired and refreshed." ✣

Reading and Writing *(opposite)* The newly renovated bedroom is furnished with a tufted bench covered in Clarence House suede by Fitzgerald. The bedcovering, found in Istanbul, was inspired by an old Ottoman design.

Guests' Delight *(above)* The small room, which opens onto the terrace, serves both as Paul Vincent Wiseman's office and as a charming guest room. On the overscale late Victorian secretary stand plaster busts of Roman emperors and Roman antiquities.

LYRIC FANTASY

TOM *and* LINDA SCHEIBAL*s' house overlooking Calistoga*

———

"LAND IN THE NAPA VALLEY HAS BECOME SO PRECIOUS AND SO PURSUED THAT YOU HAVE TO BUILD SOMETHING WORTHY OF THE APPELLATION", SAID FURNITURE DESIGNER TOM SCHEIBAL, WHO RECENTLY COMPLETED THE RENOVATION AND redesign of a Calistoga house built in 1940 by a retired French naval captain.

Scheibal, originally from the Pacific Northwest, has lived in the northern Napa Valley since 1979, when he closed his San Francisco antiques shop and headed for a quieter life in the wine country. At that time, the Napa Valley was a rather sleepy agricultural region with just a few dedicated winemakers, a handful of exceptional wines, and only the distant dream of being a summer haunt and chic destination. From Napa to Calistoga and into the Alexander Valley, even in the early eighties there were no world-class cuisine, vineyard weddings, gourmet groceries, or fashion and style stores. The arrival of Thomas Keller and his French Laundry, which opened little more than a decade ago, changed all that.

Three years ago, by then firmly planted in the valley, Tom Scheibal went looking for a new property. He had sold an old farmhouse and searched for three months for an estate with character and privacy. "I had almost given up when a friend remarked that she had seen a real estate agent nailing a For Sale sign on a fence that morning," said Scheibal. "I raced up to the house, which is on a hillside overlooking Calistoga, only to find six other eager buyers."

The house, in spite of Scheibal's optimism, was surrounded by a parched garden, a sea of beer bottles, and an incomplete renovation that left the attic and upstairs bedrooms in a shambles. The gravel driveway, whipped into a dust storm by each arriving car, ended right at the front door. Still, Scheibal saw possibilities.

Dappled Light *(opposite)* On the dining terrace, which is just outside the living room doors, the Scheibals have arranged iron and cast-aluminum furniture designed by Tom and made in Baja, Mexico. "The doors open straight onto the terrace, so we often enjoy breakfast, lunch, and dinner out on the terrace in summer," said Tom. The terrace is shaded by Japanese maple trees, Douglas firs, and manzanitas and scented by mock orange trees in terra-cotta pots and a profusion of white geraniums.

Beckoning Us Close *(above)* A pair of nineteenth-century Venetian blackamoors dance on each side of the French limestone fireplace in the living room. Tom Scheibal designed the pair of camelback sofas, inspired by a traditional French design he had seen in a château in the South of France. They're slipcovered in natural cotton canvas with a silhouette of black piping. The nineteenth-century Maine lead and bronze arrow weathervane stands on a glass-topped iron table, a Giacometti spin-off by Scheibal, crafted in Mexico. The clear fir beams, newly added to the house to give the rooms heft, were white-washed and sanded for an antique patina.

Distant Drummer *(opposite)* The floor in the living room is travertine with twelve-inch pine planks. A pair of red leather chairs, bought at Macy's in San Francisco, are poised next to a vintage Calistoga High School marching band drum with a cowhide top, which Tom Scheibal set on an iron base. The 1880 Italian saint figure, sans gown and halo, was acquired from an antique shop in Bruges, Belgium.

"The house is close to town, so I could walk into Calistoga, and it has six acres of trees, so I would have endless privacy," he said. He could envision a small French château, a bit eccentric, in the green landscape, with old madrone trees and an apple and pear orchard.

Tom and his wife, Linda Scheibal, a musician, lived in an elegant barn while he worked on the house for a year with the contractors. Workers installed new ceiling beams in the living and dining rooms to give them distinction and definition. Scheibal realigned all the rooms, finished the walls in hand-troweled plaster, installed a new kitchen and bathrooms, and ended up repairing every surface.

"The saving grace was the limestone fireplace in the living room and the travertine and pine plank floors, which I cleaned up," he said. Scheibal added French doors on three sides of the living room.

"My guiding principle was a French-style retreat, without the château clichés, in honor of the French captain," said Scheibal. "He installed the slate roof, which has beautiful lines, and his siting of the house on the mountain was impeccable."

Scheibal marvels at the French dignitary setting down roots in the Calistoga region, which was known most for its curative spas and medicinal mineral waters at the time.

"This was a major style statement he made, bringing provincial France to Northern California," he noted.

The couple furnished the house with their worldly collections of Italian, French, and American antiques, along with a fine group of California plein air paintings and furniture designed by Tom.

The house is a congenial and stylish setting for family weddings, dinners for forty guests, and opera aria performances by visiting Italian singers.

Daughter Meghan Scheibal, a mezzo-soprano, is studying voice in Italy, and her sister, Blaire, is an actor in New York City. Son Quinn and his wife, Emily, design and craft cement urns and garden ornaments.

"Between all their friends and our extended family, there is always music in the house," said Scheibal. "I'm so glad I took a chance on this property. We will be here for a long time, with music and laughter." ❧

Summer Roses (opposite) The dining room has a view to the Palisades and Mount St. Helena, in the northern reaches of the Napa Valley, beyond the town of Calistoga. Tom Scheibal, who formerly owned furniture stores in St. Helena and Calistoga, had the Louis XVI-style chairs crafted and gilded in Mexico. He turned a painter's drop cloth into a tablecloth and finished it with a painted border. The floor is travertine with pine planks. A handcrafted glass vase holds an armful of heirloom roses, a tribute to the Mexican colonial bearded and painted saint, found in Oaxaca, Mexico. The antique mirror is Italian.

LOFTY PURSUITS

Artist WADE HOEFER'*s loft in Healdsburg*

———

WITH ITS WORLDLY COLLECTIONS OF PARISIAN CHANDELIERS, SPANISH ANTIQUES, FRENCH FORTIES LEATHER CLUB CHAIRS, WITTY OBJETS TROUVÉS, AND A BRAVURA DISPLAY OF HIS OWN LARGE-SCALE PAINTINGS AND SCULPTURE, WADE HOEFER'S chic live-in loft feels as if it's in the heart of Barcelona or perhaps sunny Avignon. But it's in the middle of a noted wine-growing region, one hour north of the Golden Gate Bridge. Surprisingly, it is just a block from the leafy plaza in Healdsburg—above a bustling shopping center.

"There are no role models for an artist's country loft in California, so I was free to please myself with the decor," said Hoefer. "The space was open to interpretation. I've always seen it as a great adventure and experiment," said the artist. "I painted the walls in a neutral gray/sage palette and fashioned comfortable spaces that are flexible and practical."

His painting studio is at the back of the loft. There he paints his limpid, idyllic oils of poetic landscapes, dusk-lit lakes, and billowing clouds. Hoefer's lyrical landscape paintings, some of them propped casually against the walls, enrich the dramatic architecture. His large canvases, monoprints, triptychs, and collages are shown at the John Berggruen Gallery in San Francisco and at the Patricia Faure Gallery in Santa Monica.

The four-thousand-square-foot loft's artful interior design, illuminated by twenty-one skylights, juxtaposes a large-scale Mexican steel-framed mirror against a black-lacquered antique Chinese table, and contrasts thirties Thonet dining chairs and wild branches of pokeweed with the monochromatic gray/sage/taupe color scheme. Horsehair-filled twenties leather club chairs jostle elegant linen-covered slipper chairs in the style of Billy Baldwin.

"When you have such a malleable space, the best approach is to keep it simple, but that does not mean boring," said Wade. "This space is very liberating, and I made comfort a priority. I wanted a sophisticated mood beneath the fourteen-foot-high ceilings."

An Artist's Loft Redefined (opposite) Rooms in the loft are defined by art and furniture groups. A steel table from Oly Studio centers a seating arrangement. The tall wire jar lamp was designed by Ron Mann.

Inspired Art (left) Sunlight filters in through twenty-one ribbed-glass skylights, which illuminate Hoefer's paintings as well as his artful vignettes. The painted Chinese balsawood table was acquired from San Francisco antiques dealer Lawrence Maloney. The floor is waxed ten-inch-thick pine planks, salvaged from an old building in San Francisco.

Open Wide (opposite) Hoefer's dramatic loft, with its soaring ceiling, diffused light, and neutral color scheme, serves as elegant and meditative living quarters, studio, and private gallery for his virtuoso art works. Built out in the top floor of a former supermarket, the space expresses the ideals of creative reuse. The sofas are slipcovered in Belgian linen.

The loft was a lucky discovery. In search of a well-lit studio fifteen years ago, the artist found the 110-foot-long raw space, which had been built beneath the reinforced concrete ceiling of a forties Purity supermarket. The first floor below the loft was redeveloped into offices and shops.

With its arched concrete ceiling that curves overhead, his loft feels at once modern and timeless. For a while Wade painted there in splendid solitude. A few years later, he and his wife, interior designer Myra Hoefer, built a series of ten-feet-high walls to enclose a luxurious new bathroom, an office, and a small bedroom.

Linen-covered sofas, black lacquer tables, and Oly Studio zinc tables that hold drinks and books, keep the space suave and soothing. On the hottest days of summer, the air-conditioning kicks in, and the loft remains cool and calm.

The paled-down colors also provide the perfect background for Wade's dramatic tabletop vignettes. Quirky found objects and bowls of fruit and vegetables from the town's Saturday farmers' market add life and texture. Hoefer recycled rusted feed troughs as elegantly curved console tables.

One addition to the loft was a handsome pine plank floor that sweeps down the length of the space like an emphatic brushstroke.

"I wanted something solid underfoot," said Wade, who travels to Aspen, Santa Barbara, Paris, and Los Angeles for shows, for inspiration, and for art research.

His loft is now a territory few would want to leave. Every corner holds pleasure for the eye. "An open loft like this should not get too cluttered, so I edit the collections and keep the focus on my paintings," noted Wade. "Everything is visible, from one end to the other so I protect the symmetry and sightlines."

The poetry of the place is not lost on the artist.

"It's very private and surprisingly silent," noted Wade, who grew up in Southern California. "I begin the morning with the music of Tito Schipa, Erik Satie, or Bill Evans, and progress to Paolo Conte's songs or Nils Petter Molvaer's *Khmer*. Jacques Brel lifts the mood in the afternoon."

Fresh Spirit (*above and opposite*) The black lacquered X-leg table was crafted by Wade Hoefer, inspired by a Christian Liaigre design. Birch Thonet chairs were found in Carnac, Brittany. The Daliesque silver-gilt chandelier was from 21 Arrondissement in Healdsburg.

Bold Gestures *(above)* A pair of twenties French club chairs stuffed with their original horsehair make fine company for a wire jar lamp by Ron Mann. The shade is parchment.

Open Mind *(opposite)* The Palladium bed was acquired through the Room & Board catalog. "The loft feels like a retreat and a threshold on which to set off on an art journey," said Wade.

Perhaps best of all, when they first moved in, Wade and Myra tamed their wildest fantasies and kept construction to a minimum. Islands of comfort for eating, sleeping, working, and painting are simply defined by screens, large sofas, conversation groups of chairs, and paintings.

Works in progress take their cues from Wade's weeks of painting on the Costa Brava. After a summer sojourn painting there, Wade began sketching new ceramic designs and paintings that are lighter and more abstract.

"The loft will continue to evolve, and my paintings always move forward," he said. "I'm content with the loft's background tones of pale gray, stone, lichen, ocher, and sage. They don't compete with my paintings." ❧

Natural Instincts (left) Naturally shed mule deer antlers found beneath aspen trees in Nevada are clustered in a broken French olive oil jar. The forged-iron lamp is by Sonoma designer Ron Mann. The Fenestra paintings were created for the Patricia Faure Gallery in Santa Monica.

Grace in Action (right) Artist Wade Hoefer at his canvas illuminated by soft light from a skylight. His studio, in the center of the town of Healdsburg, in Sonoma County, is soundproof and private, thanks to mid-century construction of a curved concrete roof. His building was a former Purity grocery. Hoefer paints a range of images, including poetic landscapes, clouds that seem to billow forth from the canvas, historical California icons, and riverscapes as profound, timeless, and moving as religious iconography. His newest canvases were inspired by the Catalonian countryside. Hoefer's paintings are available through the John Berggruen Gallery in San Francisco and the Patricia Faure Gallery in Santa Monica.

CONFIDENTLY MODERNE

DAVE DeMATTEI *and* PATRICK WADE
commute from San Francisco to their weekend retreat in St. Helena

———

FOR MORE THAN TEN YEARS, PATRICK WADE, A SENIOR VICE PRESIDENT, CREATIVE, FOR WILLIAMS-SONOMA EMERGING BRANDS, AND DAVE DEMATTEI, PRESIDENT OF THE COMPANY, WERE DEEPLY IMMERSED IN THEIR PROFESSIONAL LIVES IN NEW YORK City. They lived in a spacious loft in SoHo, and on Friday evenings they headed for Southampton to relax in their classic saltbox house not far from the beach.

DeMattei and Wade also kept their handsome Edwardian house in San Francisco, planning eventually to return to the West Coast to spend time with their families. In 2003 they headed back to California and acquired a house with twelve acres of garden and vineyards on Napa Valley's western edge, the highly regarded region known to winemakers and growers as the Rutherford Bench.

The partners' property came with a certain prestige: this benchland of warm alluvial soil and hot summers yields much of the best Cabernet Sauvignon in California. The area's twenty-five hundred acres of gently sloping vineyards are home to Cabernet Sauvignon grapes that are selected by premium labels like Robert Mondavi, Joseph Phelps, Beaulieu, Heitz Wine Cellars (Martha's Vineyard and Bella Oaks bottlings are from the Rutherford Bench), Inglenook, Grgich Hills, Opus One, Far Niente, Sequoia Grove, and Cakebread.

"We loved the idea of being surrounded by working farms and great grapes," said Patrick Wade, who grew up in Oregon. Their house is situated on a quiet road lined with fragrant eucalyptus trees, white oleanders, and vineyards.

The property included a redwood grove, a vineyard of Cabernet grapes, a croquet lawn, a *potager*, a swimming pool, and a guesthouse/garage.

"The house had such potential, even though it was a seventies ranch house that had been transmogrified into the banal Tuscan villa," said Wade. "We knew we could turn it into a low-key, sunny retreat, a place where we could garden, entertain, and get away from the city."

Weekend Arrangements (opposite) Patrick Wade and Dave DeMattei like the country life, but they did not intend to have a country-themed house. The modern mix includes a tall wood floor lamp with a drum shade, from West Elm, and a glass-topped table with an ebonized wood base from March, San Francisco. The fireplace is French limestone. The cashmere throws are from Williams-Sonoma Home.

They first drew up a new landscape design with Napa Valley landscape architect Steven Dailey. The garden would be in a classic blue-and-white palette, with Iceberg roses and lavender, framed with gnarled olive trees and privet hedges. They also decided to build a new guesthouse and personal gym, with a media room above the garage.

Wade and DeMattei had no intention of using country-style decor in their house. They reconfigured the interiors, removing walls, making rooms larger. Baseboards and mold-ings were stripped off, and the walls were plastered a pale gray-cream tone.

The color scheme for all rooms, selected for harmony and flexibility, stages rich browns, ebony, and taupe tones against pale cream, white, limestone, and eggshell. An orange cashmere throw and a kitschy cheetah print on a Pretzel chair provide surprise and contrast.

"Some of the furniture, like our leather butterfly chairs and photography, were purchased in Southampton for our beach house," noted Wade. "We wanted the interiors to feel relaxed and polished, not rustic. We liked the idea of a country house with Charles Eames chairs, shelves by Catherine Memmi, a chrome light fixture by Jonathan Adler, and a selection of pieces from the Williams-Sonoma Home catalog."

Elements of a Room (*top right, bottom right, and opposite*) Patrick Wade has a perfect sense of composition and contrast. In the living room, he juxtaposed a tall, sculptural West Elm floor lamp with angular leather stools in chrome and leather, from Williams-Sonoma Home. The glass-topped table is from March, San Francisco. At one end of the living room, he arranged a mid-century vignette with a Jean Prouvé desk (missing a drawer), a Charles Eames spool-shaped low table, an adjustable brushed nickel lamp from Williams-Sonoma Home, and a kitschy fifties chair, which he covered in a faux-cheetah printed chenille.

They stripped down rooms to give them a modern air and cleaned up fittings and fixtures to freshen the interiors. Simplifying the interiors also made them very low maintenance.

"On Friday nights, we leave the office and drive up to St. Helena and always meet friends at Press Restaurant for dinner," said Wade. "Saturday mornings, we're in our shorts, walking in the garden, checking on the vegetables and herbs, breathing in the scent of lavender and grapes and fragrant valley air. Some weekends we don't leave the property. We might drive in to St. Helena for breakfast, and a glance over Erin Martin's design store. We swim, cook dinner on the grill, garden, work out, and at the end of the day we open a bottle of Cabernet Sauvignon from the region. It's a blast. And best of all, on Sunday night, if we time it right, we're only a little more than a hour from home." 🐾

Relaxed Dining (opposite) The Nassau dining table, of bamboo, is from Williams-Sonoma Home. Charles Eames dining chairs have dark walnut-stained seats and backs. The painted Chippendale-style chair is from Jonathan Adler, and the shelves are from Catherine Memmi in Paris.

Garden Views (left and above) The property includes more than twenty olive trees, a rose garden with heirloom roses, espaliered fruit trees, a vineyard planted to Cabernet Sauvignon grapes, raised vegetable beds, and lavish rows of fragrant lavender. From their terrace, Wade and DeMattei have panoramic views of the Rutherford Bench, the Mayacamas Range, and perfectly groomed vineyards.

California

RETREATS

——

Je rêve d'un logie, maison basse à fenêtres

Hautes, aux trois degrès usées, plats, et verdis

Logie secret à l'air d'antique estampe

Qui ne vit qu'en moi-même, où je rentre parfois

M'asseoir et oublier le jour gris et la pluie.

I dream of a house, a low house with high

Windows, three worn steps, smooth and green

A secret house, as in an old print,

That lives only in me, where sometimes I return

To sit down and forget the gray day, and the rain.

❧

ANDRÉ LAFON [1883–1915]

from *La Maison Pauvre, Poèmes,*

Temps Présent

COUNTRY FOLLY

IRA YEAGER's pavilion near Calistoga, Napa Valley

———

IN THE WILD GREEN HILLS NORTH OF CALISTOGA, ARTIST IRA YEAGER HAS BUILT A PLEASURE PAVILION FOR ART, MUSIC, LAVISH FEASTS, AND SUMMER FROLIC. STEP INTO HIS DREAMY GUSTAVIAN-STYLE COUNTRY HOUSE, AND IT'S LIKE TRIPPING into the eighteenth century. Yeager greets guests wearing a handsome nipped-waist cutaway crimson jacket made in 1776 for a French nobleman. He reposes on a languorous down-filled Provençal chaise longue, dines on elegant French porcelain plates, and displays his French silver teapot on a superb French marquetry desk.

Yeager happily admits that he is obsessed with eighteenth-century France. So much so that he paints lively scenes and portraits inspired by that fabled French century, and he surrounds himself with eighteenth-century French antique cabinets and gueridons, portraits, and objets (shipped from France by his dear friend, antiques dealer Lillian Williams).

After leaving his San Francisco studio to live and paint in the wine country ten years ago, Yeager came upon a neglected walnut orchard in a remote valley north of Calistoga. He decided to build a country Swedish cottage in the Gustavian style. This neoclassical style, which flowered in Stockholm in the late eighteenth century, was directly inspired by the eighteenth-century architecture and decor fashionable in France at the time of Louis XVI, a hero of Yeager's.

To help Yeager realize his dream, his friend Calistoga architect Richard Horwath limned a charming board-and-batten structure with a soaring ceiling and stripped-pine support columns.

On his colorful, gestural canvases Yeager paints into existence the romantic European world he wishes to inhabit. With equal Francophile intensity, he builds and decorates the eighteenth-century Europe in which he wishes to dwell. He signs some paintings "von Yäger 1785" in the manner of Swedish court painters of the time of King Gustav III.

Homage to King Gustav *(opposite)* A nineteenth-century French neoclassical dining table with a *faux marbre* top is encircled by a handsome series of Gustavian-style chairs. An unpainted eighteenth-century Swedish commode stands beside the peeled-pine trunk column, ornamented with a painted Italian mirror. The handcrafted carpet is Chinese.

Country Idyll (*opposite*) Yeager's bravura painting of a deer, inspired by the denizens of his Calistoga country property, dominates a corner of his Gustavian folly. An elegant antique French armoire, painted with country motifs, is accompanied by a French hay-barn ladder and a decorative *chauffeuse*, a French chair positioned with a low seat, designed to pull close to the fireplace. The antique striped rug is Swedish.

The Passionate Collector (*left*) Ira Yeager created a deskscape of a Meissen porcelain cabbage, an eighteenth-century French teapot, and a French porcelain lemon on a finely crafted French desk in noble eighteenth-century French garb.

Happy Daze (*above*) An antique Italian stone cherub, one of a pair, casts his happy smile on Ira Yeager's terrace overlooking vineyards and walnut groves north of Calistoga.

"I admire and appreciate everything French and eighteenth-century Swedish," said Yeager, who studied painting in Paris while in his twenties. "The eighteenth century was a golden era in France and Sweden—the blossoming of design, courtly life, fashion, art, music, and culture. I'm curious about what it all means. I paint characters of that period and collect the antiques so that I can understand that century and come face-to-face with the philosophy and daily life."

Yeager has been making his mark on the San Francisco art scene since the fifties. He grew up in Bellingham, Washington, and studied art first at the California College of Arts and Crafts and later at the San Francisco Art Institute with early teachers

such as Richard Diebenkorn, Nathan Oliveira, and Elmer Bischoff. In the sixties and seventies, Yeager studied and painted in Italy, Paris, and Morocco and lived for a decade on the Greek island of Corfu.

"The Napa Valley is a wonderful place for an artist," said Yeager. "It's relaxed and incredibly beautiful through the seasons. I can disappear for days and throw myself into my paintings, or I can head down Highway 29 to the French Laundry or the Swanson Winery salon and be very social. I might drive over to the St. Helena Olive Oil Company to buy the best olive oil in the world. Here everything is possible in the best of all possible worlds, as Voltaire said."

The pale-gray Gustavian folly, surrounded by five acres of flourishing walnut trees encrusted with pale green lichen, makes for a dramatic bucolic scene, with deer nibbling tender grass shoots and doves nesting among the gnarled oaks. Yeager's art today is passionately engaging, but it's clear that the true métier of this painter is the past.

The present is picture-perfect. But for Ira Yeager there is always his brush with the golden and glorious eighteenth century. ❧

Light and Repose (*left*) An antique Provençal *méridienne* upholstered in traditional French printed cotton accompanies a nineteenth-century French painted table, a painted English tole tray, and a pair of Yeager's oil paintings depicting spirited creatures dressed.

French Evolution (*opposite*) Ira Yeager studied painting in Paris for several years, and has never given up his deep love of French history and aesthetics. He collects eighteenth-century French costumes, French porcelains, French crystal, and the perfect French relaxed design ideals.

ARCADIAN DAYS

RICHARD ANDERSON *and* BRANDON BURG'*s cottage near the Russian River*

———

THE PARADOX OF SUMMER IN SAN FRANCISCO IS THAT WHILE EVERYONE IMAGINES THE COAST BASKING IN FULL-ON CALIFORNIA SUNSHINE, THE CITY BY THE BAY IS SEQUESTERED IN SILVERY FOG. MARINE MISTS, WHICH CREEP IN TO THE sound of lowing foghorns, cast a cool, still mood over the city. After a few July weekends of gray, chill, and sunless torpor, residents in search of heat drive across the Golden Gate Bridge and head for all points north and east.

San Francisco interior designer Richard Anderson and his partner, software analyst Brandon Burg, were spurred on to find their summer escape route by the arrival of two beloved rescued pound puppies, Parker and Daisy.

"We wanted a weekend house for our dogs so that they could run free," said Anderson, a partner with Candra Scott & Anderson, a design firm that specializes in historical restoration of hotels around the country. "We dreamed of a summer escape route so that we could all enjoy the legendary California summers."

A few years ago, Anderson and Burg went in search of an affordable country fixer-upper.

"The property had to be less than a hundred miles from the city, so that we could easily drive there on Friday night and arrive in time for a relaxed dinner, and make a fast and easy drive home on Sunday night," said Anderson. The partners' first concept was a remote country house where they could escape city cares.

"We did Internet searches and would make day trips into Sonoma County, talk to realtors," said Anderson.

Their focus turned to Monte Rio in Sonoma County, not far from the town of Guerneville. The region is known for its redwood groves and for notable wines like the sparkling ones produced by Iron Horse Winery.

From the Redwood Forest (opposite) Richard Anderson designed two new redwood branch pavilions overlooking the Russian River and groves of redwoods. In the dining pavilion, vintage table and twenties chairs by the Old Hickory Furniture Company invite guests to enjoy fresh salads, corn on the cob, and fried chicken. The ten-by-ten-foot pavilions were crafted from tree branches lopped from redwoods on the property. "We left them *au natural* so that they would look as if they'd been there for decades," said Anderson. A second pavilion is used as an outdoor sitting room, with a Lloyd loom sofa upholstered in vintage cotton canvas awning fabric. The weather is clear and sunny every summer day, and it never rains from May through November, so the furniture is left outdoors for months at a time.

Fourth of July Revels *(left)* The Russian River towns, like small towns throughout the United States, celebrate the Fourth of July with enthusiasm. Anderson and Burg invite their city-slicker friends for a jolt of Americana—complete with knotty pine walls, rag rugs, and flags.

Flea-market Finds *(above)* Anderson often spends weekends searching through swap meets and estate sales to find the vintage Americana objects and textiles he prefers. He found the turquoise-painted table in a San Francisco antiques mall. The Monterey vintage painted wood lamp was discovered in an antiques shop in Spokane, Washington. Three decal-decorated bark vases are Adirondack tourist souvenirs.

Camps and Cottages *(right)* Anderson and Burg planted cottage-style shrubs and flowers, including pink hydrangeas, around their river retreat.

Monte Rio's small-town America assets include the Rio, a first-run cinema in a Quonset hut, and a neon sign above the main street boasting in Technicolor "Welcome to Monte Rio Vacation Wonderland."

In the twenties and thirties, the summer crowds were attracted to the big bands, which played dance music into the night. Towns had roller rinks, dance halls, and a sense of summer glamour.

"We finally found our house in Monte Rio by chance, on a flyer tacked to a fence," recalled Anderson. "It was a poorly built fifties cottage, with not much sense of design. It was the least expensive house we saw, and even though the interiors were dark and depressing,

we could see the possibilities. It was 'the little house that could.' We bought it. And we named it Dogwood, in honor of our pets."

The cottage, measuring six hundred square feet, stands in a clearing on a bluff high above the Russian River. The narrow quarter-acre lot offers easy access to the river. They built a dock, where they keep a canoe, also named Dogwood.

Though they faced the discouragements of aluminum windows, an overgrown garden, and dark rooms with vinyl fake-wood floors, they had a vision.

Anderson was drawn to create an Adirondack camp-style cottage beneath the redwood trees.

"Our first weekend, we demolished the interior, pulled out the kitchen, the bathroom, and the faux-wood walls and the faux-wood floor coverings," Anderson said. His design concept was to take the house back in time to the twenties, a time of idyllic river cottages, when trains took glamorous groups of city dwellers to weekend frivolity.

Dogs' Paradise (opposite) A vintage forties Coronado armchair with hand-painted flowers was upholstered in vinyl, with a vintage blanket woven with a Native American motif. A circular rag rug found at the Alameda Flea Market swirls around the octagonal Del Rey table.

Sweet Retreat (left) Richard Anderson designed cotton ticking in the bedroom for a forties vintage look. The designer and his business partner, designer Candra Scott, focus their practice on redesigning and re-creating historic hotels, and they collect rare vintage textiles, hand-crafted antiques, and eccentric examples of Americana. Among the treasures: vintage needlepoint dog pillows. The knotty-pine wall paneling is new, crafted to look old. The bedside lamps are from the twenties.

Anderson and Burg installed new wood-framed mullion windows and painted them green, so that they would seem original to the one-bedroom house.

They hired an arborist to trim surrounding redwood trees to let in more sunlight and fresh air. In front of the house, and overlooking the river, they built a pair of rustic outdoor pavilions using the unpeeled and untrimmed twigs.

During more than six months of remodeling, the partners installed new wide-plank floors stained golden brown. They added tongue-in-groove knotty-pine interior walls, which were crafted and shellacked and hand finished to look as if they'd been in the house for eighty years.

The period decor includes Del Rey, Coronado, and Monterey Western-style furniture, twig tables, and Adirondack bark souvenir vases. The kitchen celebrated an earlier no-cares era with a new red Formica counter-top, a vintage Wedgewood stove, a vintage Hotpoint refrigerator, and collections of vintage Bauer bowls.

"It's small and compact and incredibly comfortable for a weekend visit," said Anderson. "The setting is magnificent. After all our work, and the dust and upheaval of taking the cabin down to the floorboards, we can finally enjoy it."

Friends drive up for a day of sunbathing and canoe-ing. The dogs frolic and lie around contentedly for hours. After lunch, there's a lull. Hours pass in drowsy bliss.

"The Fourth of July celebrations are old-fashioned Americana and include a parade of boats on the river, fireworks displays, and family picnics complete with apple pies and barbecue," noted Anderson. "We now know lots of families, and we invite our friends to come for lunch and dinner. It's hot and sunny, and the air is still and so relaxed. It's like stepping back decades to early California. Best of all, our dogs love it." ✺

Life on the River (above) Anderson and Burg built a pair of garden pavilions so that they could dine and relax in the shade, with the sound of the Russian River murmuring below.

Escape from the Twenty-first Century (opposite) Anderson likes to keep his dining pavilion rustic and relaxed.

INTO THE WILDS

JED POGRAN *and* GARY MCGREGOR'*s retreat in the Anderson Valley*

———

JED POGRAN, PRESIDENT OF GUMP'S, THE VENERABLE STYLE AND DESIGN STORE IN DOWNTOWN SAN FRANCISCO SINCE THE GOLD RUSH DAYS, WOULD SEEM TO BE THE CONSUMMATE CITY GENTLEMAN. DAPPER AND DEBONAIR, HE'S A LIFELONG connoisseur of art, classical jazz, and city life. A few years ago, Pogran and his partner, Gary McGregor, a lighting designer, went for a jaunt in the Anderson Valley, visited friends, explored around the small towns of Philo and Navarro, and eventually acquired fifteen acres bordering a national forest preserve. The land, mostly native trees and hillsides sloping down to a creek, had never been developed.

The Anderson Valley, just over one hundred miles north of San Francisco, was first settled in the 1840s, around the time of the Gold Rush. After a checkered history (prohibition, planting the wrong crops and grapes, feuds with the Pomo tribe, the challenges of transporting fruit from this remote location to Ukiah and San Francisco, the fates of the logging industry) the fifteen-mile-long valley is now a highly regarded wine-growing region. More than twenty-five winemakers, including the highly regarded Roederer Estate, Scharffenberger Cellars, Greenwood Ridge, Navarro Vineyards, and Husch now give the valley its character.

Winters there, just miles from the Mendocino coast and surrounded by noble, dramatic redwood forests, are cold and foggy. In springtime late frosts often bite the valley floor, so the Anderson Valley climate is considered one of the coolest for successful commercial grape growing. Nevertheless, wineries thrive, and new acreage and new grape varieties (Pinot Gris) are planted every year.

Pogran and McGregor felt at home in hidden corners of the valley and eventually began planning a retreat they could drive to from the city each weekend.

Home Away from Home (opposite and following page) Jed Pogran and Gary McGregor built their weekend retreat based on historical farmhouses in the Anderson Valley. The exterior, which has a ten-foot-wide wraparound porch, is finished in drop-lap siding. The window frames feature a dark-bronze finish metal. Pogran and McGregor's property borders a national preserve, and they decided to let the forest and woodlands be their garden, in effect, choosing not to impose a new landscape on their hillside. Pogran and McGregor visit the house most weekends throughout the year.

Pogran even loves the implacable curves and switchbacks between Highway 101 and Yorkville that deter many a weekend driver.

"That winding drive, which gives many people vertigo, is one of the most beautiful in America," he said. "The Anderson Valley is rustic and truly rural, and not at all chichi."

Pogran and McGregor installed a well and cleared fallen trees. They hired San Francisco architect Ira Kurlander to plan the house, which was carefully positioned midway along a south-facing slope, facing an ocean of redwood and fir trees.

"The plan was to work within the vernacular of traditional farmhouses and agricultural buildings in the valley," said Pogran. "We chose a standing seam galvanized steel roof, almost standard for barns and farm buildings, and the drop-lap siding."

Pogran focused from the start on a practical building that would be both a welcoming retreat where they could arrive and at once feel at home and a house they could just leave, lock the doors and gates, and never be concerned that a rainstorm, roaming deer, or frost might create havoc.

Four-inch-round galvanized downspouts and six-inch galvanized gutters were dictated by the local lore

and are both hardworking and harmonious. The porch was built with reclaimed old-growth redwood, scavenged by a local source.

"When the valley was first logged, the timber was so abundant that old-growth stumps that were too hard to remove and logs that were impossible to drag out were simply abandoned," noted Pogran. His lumber dealer retrieves those treasures.

The Color Green (opposite and above) New York color consultant Jack Burris worked with Pogran and McGregor on the color scheme for their entire house. He selected a soft sage green for the chair rail with a softer shade of green below it, to give the effect of a wainscot. An oak table from Gump's, a dramatic bentwood rocking chair, and vintage lamps from Palmer Hargrave (one of the Dessin Fournir luxury furniture and accessories) are among their carefully chosen furnishings. The sofa and ottoman, covered in a Henry Calvin cotton, is from Crate & Barrel. The interiors include old restored doors, simple moldings, and antique cabinet hardware. A Danish firebox stands on a sheet of sandblaster steel.

This passionate timber dealer milled the recovered wood into tongue-in-groove floor planks for the porch. He also provided milled old timber for the porch rails and posts.

"We wanted redwood, which is so much part of the history of the valley," noted Pogran. "But we could not see killing off a fifteen-hundred-year-old tree for our house. Reclaiming these timbers is the best kind of ecology."

Restraint is everything for Pogran and McGregor. The porch rails could not be simpler. At four by six inches, the top rail is wide enough to sit on, and the upright boards, four inches across, are as plain as can be.

"We wanted the house to feel contemporary but ambiguous, not fakey old," said Pogran.

The house is an essay on making a solid, substantial place that feels attached to the land, without a feeling of pretentiousness. The fifteen-hundred-square-foot house has two bedrooms, a small kitchen with a walnut-stained floor, and a living room/dining room. New York color consultant Jack Burris worked up a palette of pale greens for the interior. McGregor designed the lighting.

To Sleep, Perchance to Dream (*opposite and above*) Pogran found the vintage American spindle bed at the Alameda Flea Market, a favorite of San Francisco area decorators and antiques dealers, who work their way through hundreds of stands to find a broad range of well-priced decor.

"We love the spring when the fields and hillsides are vibrant blue and orange with lupines and California poppies," said Pogran. "Every time of year is thrilling in the Anderson Valley. We drive down our road, lock the gate, and seldom leave except perhaps to buy fresh salmon from the local fishermen. We don't watch television. We have only an old TV for watching DVDs on a rainy night."

The longtime partners often work in the garden until dark, carrying rocks up from the creek to create natural landscaping around the figs and cutting garden.

They have planted native trees, including toyon, redwood, native maples, alders, western hazelnuts, and dogwoods. Local high school students harvest acorns from their trees and germinate them, and Pogran buys them back and plants the saplings.

"We are totally obsessed with turning the woodlands into a beautifully groomed natural place," he said. "Planting all these trees forces you to think long-term. We want to grow old here, savor the seasons. Like 'Capability' Brown in England, we have the sense of stewardship. This land will look its best in fifty to two hundred years."

They park their car beneath the oaks and approach the house along a gravel path and across a mown field.

"It's much more romantic than driving straight up to the house," said Pogran. "It has a feeling of a house in a grassy meadow, a hunting lodge, a Zen retreat."

They are close to nature, and in touch with the seasons. "There we found the real world, nature at its best," Pogran said. ✖

Country Manners (left and opposite) Pogran and McGregor like to leave the world behind when they drive to their Mendocino County cabin on weekends. Still, style matters, so they've decorated the rooms with vintage finds like their clock from the Alameda flea market, a hand-blown glass vase from Gump's, and a painted chicken. Their sculptural dining table and Queen Anne–style chairs were also vintage finds. The men keep the interiors simple and very low-maintenance so that they can come and go with light hearts.

WEEKEND ROMANCE

DANE WILSON's cottage in the Russian River Valley

———

SAN FRANCISCO INTERIOR DESIGNER DANE WILSON'S SUNNY APARTMENT ON RUSSIAN HILL IS TRANQUIL, AND THE 1880-ERA FLAT IS BEAUTIFULLY DETAILED WITH MARBLE FIREPLACES, HANDSOME STAIRWAYS, AND HAND-WAXED HARDWOOD floors. There Dane is surrounded by his collection of vintage glass, photography, and antiques, some of them treasures from his youthful days as a sidewalk scavenger, finding a castaway Hans Wegner chair in Pacific Heights, and rescuing a curvaceous wing chair with carved legs on the streets of Nob Hill. On a midnight run on Russian Hill long ago, he came upon a fine oak pedestal table, which he painted white. Decorator's luck.

One chilly Saturday in July, as he sat perched in his bay window high above Chinatown enjoying the view of the Bay Bridge, Dane decided that he wanted to get out of the city on weekends to a place where the sun shines all summer long and where he could face new decorating challenges.

"I love city life, but I suddenly dreamed of Mendocino, the Anderson Valley, a change of scenery, a different house, blue skies," he said.

He quickly got over the dramatic Mendocino coast, deterred by the three-hour drive and winding roads. Closer to the city, he started talking to real estate agents in the Russian River Valley and began looking at properties around Forestville.

"It's a charming community along the Gravenstein Highway," noted Wilson.

Forestville is a blink-of-an-eye town, with a hardware store and a handful of art galleries. Rustic and sun-dappled, it is starting to regain the heyday it enjoyed in the early twenties, when summer camps sprang up and the Russian River and redwood forests beckoned with an only-in-California allure.

Tree Time (opposite) Built in 1915, the retreat has a black and green shingled exterior, white painted wood window frames, and the green frame of noble redwoods, tan oaks, and California bay trees.

Eight miles west of town, perched above the river in a century-old community of summer houses, Wilson discovered a 1915 shingled cottage with casement windows. Standing in a clearing with views of the river, it was a diamond in the rough with all the right architectural elements, but all the wrong paint colors, as well as odd room and door placements. It had been in one family for generations.

"I saw an old neglected Franklin stove sitting on the porch, and a bathroom that's accessible only through the garden, a very indoor/outdoor experience," said Dane of his first visit. He was seduced by the stillness beneath the redwoods, the fragrance of bay and balsam that hovered in the air, and by an old house longing to be polished and given a new life.

Peering through the dust motes, he saw stained-glass windows, casement windows, romantic river views, and lots of character. Beneath the old carpets and improvised pole closets, he found a three-bedroom cottage with space for weekend guests, and a carefree air.

"I decided to turn it into my own version of an old summer camp house and to make the most of its forest setting," he said. "Within minutes I made an offer."

Wilson turned the renovation into an adventure, and a three-year work project. "My friends came up on weekends and helped me scrub and paint and clear away dust and macramé curtains and duct tape that had all held the house together for ninety years," said the designer.

Dane meticulously maintained the funkiness. "The worst mistake is to try to modernize an unpretentious house that has such integrity and dignity," he noted.

Up the River (opposite) Dane Wilson maximized the space of his ten-by-twelve-foot living room with gallons of white paint, a large antique lacquered Chinese cabinet (to conceal electronics), a Crate & Barrel leather armchair, a Wicker Works sofa, and a Brancusi-esque sculpture in palm wood, possibly made in Mexico. He found the vintage paddle beneath the house.

Weekend Cook (above) Wilson organized a weekend painting party and wielded more Kelly Moore White Shadow in the kitchen. He also added new shelves and forties tile on the countertop to achieve a new but of-the-period room.

He painted plank floors with Benjamin Moore's Danville Tan and cleaned but left intact the hand-hewn posts supporting the porch.

"I painted the walls and ceilings white to keep the interior light and bright, and to mask, somewhat, the architectural oddities," said Dane, who turns his weekend visits into a country version of his city life, going antiquing and swooping into junk shops and vintage galleries as he drives through nearby towns in search of organic vegetables and fresh bread.

In the six-by-six-foot kitchen Wilson painted all the walls white and added a new four-burner stove and an undercounter refrigerator.

"I call it my 'French' refrigerator," he said. "It's small, and I can only get a day of fresh fruit and lettuces and vegetables, like Parisian families, so we have to go and get fresh produce often."

The broad tiled counter works as a weekend bar and buffet. "I've got a juicer and a Cuisinart, so I have everything I need to make wonderful weekend feasts," said Wilson, who recently founded his own decorating firm, Dane Robert Wilson Interior Design. The late afternoon and early evening—cocktail hour on the river—is the best time in the house, said the designer, because the rooms are bright and cheerful, and the sun sweeps across the porch.

"Birds are whirring around, and at night you can hear owls," he said. "We can stargaze for hours because the air is so clear and still."

Wilson is now a Russian River devotee, and he drives up to his cottage even during the winter when rainy, misty days in the redwoods turn the whole world green and moody.

"I ended up with a wonderful weekend life, and the pleasant work of cleaning windows, cooking, sweeping leaves, and carefully clearing spiderwebs," says Wilson. "This turned into a complete escape. I immerse myself in country pursuits." The Russian River seems very far from Russian Hill. ❧

White Is Right (above and opposite) Dane Wilson painted all rooms with Kelly Moore's White Shadow to give cohesion to an interior that had been improvised, "improved," and repaired for over ninety years. A queen-size spindle bed and antique French rattan bistro chair occupy most of the bedroom. In the second bedroom, visible through the door, a John Dickinson plaster wine-jug lamp stands on an Edwardian console table.

Tree House *(above)* San Francisco interior designer Dane Wilson found his weekend cabin above the Russian River by good fortune. He and his friends spend most afternoons on the deck, lunching for hours and watching the light flicker across the trees.

Treetop Afternoon *(right)* Dane Wilson and his friends spend the weekend outdoors, and when they return from canoeing or exploring the area, they go straight to the front porch, where Dane has set up a painted dining/picnic table (original to the house) and folding French café chairs. From the porch he can see a bend in the river as it heads for the coast, fifteen miles to the west. Wilson set an armful of summer cosmos in a blown-glass pitcher to catch the afternoon sun. A white glazed ceramic table accompanies a pair of vintage rattan chairs.

COUNTRY BLISS

JOSEPHINE ALEXANDER *and* GARY AMERIGIAN *in the countryside
near Manchester, Mendicino County*

———

GARY AMERIGIAN AND JOSEPHINE ALEXANDER STILL RECALL THE 1989 EARTHQUAKE IN SAN FRANCISCO VIVIDLY. THE QUAKE AND ITS AFTERMATH WERE A SURPRISE, EVEN THERE IN EARTHQUAKE COUNTRY. THE DRAMA, THE SENSE OF vulnerability, the tragedy of lives and houses lost, and the uncertainty made them head north to their country retreat.

Alexander, a British artist originally from Edinburgh, and Amerigian, an artist/entrepreneur who spent his childhood in Sonoma County, had lived happily in San Francisco for over a decade.

"We got in the car and left San Francisco," recalled Alexander. "We wanted the solace of nature, a quiet life. We also needed more space for our studios and knew that it would be costly to find an artists' loft, or even a live-work space in the city.

"We had acquired the property in spring 1989, because we loved the lake there, and views of the ocean in the distance," said Alexander. "It's a three-hour drive up the winding coast road from San Francisco, and we never take a shortcut up the main highway."

The 130-mile trip follows a twisting and always dramatic route through the Russian River Valley, up and over coastal ridges, along wild cliff edges, through redwood groves, occasionally with fleeting views of remote and often deserted towns and untouched beaches.

Close regulation and fierce protection of these stretches of the rocky coast, along with the relative inaccessibility, have deterred development over the years. Two- or three-hour drives from the city and the region's reputation for dense summer fog have made it less attractive to weekend retreats. Beaches that draw weekend divers and offer memorable vistas for sightseers are cool and boulder strewn, and the water is chilly. The Northern California coast is not a place where sun worshipers set up cool drinks and lay out towels beneath colorful umbrellas. Hikers, abalone divers, kayakers, and long-distance cyclists are its passionate fans.

A Timeless Sense of Country (opposite) The couple finished the living room walls with white plaster tinted with natural earth pigments to give a soft ocher glow. On the white-painted antique credenza, they've arranged a pair of nineteenth-century urns filled with lavender from their garden. Among the collections on display are Italian pewter plates and a French *bouillotte* lamp with a paper shade edged in gold leaf.

"This is a land of activists who have protected and preserved the coast's natural beauty, the forests, the redwoods, the flora and fauna, and every scenic panorama," noted Alexander. "We love it even when we're driving through dense fog. When maritime mists pour across the landscape it's a silent, mysterious, and beautiful white world. You suddenly come out of this white world to hillsides drenched in sunshine, seagulls whirling, and wind-whipped waves. And there's no one around. It's perfect."

Amerigian and Alexander had acquired their house as a weekend escape, and suddenly and unexpectedly they found themselves living there full-time with no intention of returning to the city.

"You have to be self-sufficient up here near the coast," said Alexander. "We are an hour's drive from Mendocino, the nearest larger town, and except for wineries, there are no large companies where we could work."

The couple founded their company, A House in the Country, twenty-two years ago. At first, they set up their company to design and create chic European-style decorative objects like large-scale mirrors, sconces, unwired chandeliers, candlesticks, and vases inspired by the rustic objects they'd admired in the South of France.

With the arrival of the Internet, they branched out and started selling archival prints of Josephine's oil paintings of still lifes, flowers, and landscapes at trade shows and shipping to collectors around the world. Josephine is also working on a new country cookbook, illustrated with her paintings.

The house was built in 1955 as a weekend retreat, and Josephine recalls a time-warp scene of orange shag carpet and (coordinating) orange and green linoleum.

Inspiration for a Cookbook (opposite) The kitchen offers the cook an inspiring view of the cutting and herb gardens. It's built like a small European country kitchen, with everything at hand and a view of the lake in the distance. Here Josephine sears petrale sole, steams penne or fettuccine, makes a simple pasta sauce with olive oil, nutmeg, garlic, and sea salt, and roasts chicken with sage and thyme from the garden.

Far from the City (above) Weather in the coastal region is unpredictable, and even on a hot summer afternoon, brisk winds and dense fog may billow in from the ocean. The couple enclosed their terrace with redwood fencing, Cécile Brunner roses, lilies, and hydrangeas. Their Sonoma stone terrace retains heat even on a cool afternoon.

"We liked the house because the architecture was totally simple, a blank canvas," she said. "We were never deterred by the dated decor. We knew it would go."

Over the years, Gary has plastered the walls to give the house a sense of age and texture, and the couple has renovated and restyled the kitchen, added studios, installed sheltered terraces, and planted seasonal gardens. They covered the floors with terra-cotta tiles, which are cool in summer and warm in winter, and covered them with practical seagrass matting.

"We love living here because we have no intrusions, no noise, no big-city complications," said Alexander. "We walk to work, in seconds. There's no time wasted on a commute. We've never experience road rage."

The couple travels around the country to trade shows occasionally, but mostly they focus on their work.

There's time to watch the changing seasons, to smell the salty tang of fog drifting in from the coast, to enjoy the first rhododendron blooms, to take the first lilies to scent the bedroom, and other country pleasures. At night, the sky is clear. There are no streetlights to distract them from diamond-bright acres of stars.

"We love to visit the city," said Alexander. "We like to know about the new restaurants and to see our friends. But mostly we love returning home, back to our peaceful countryside. It has hardly changed in decades. That's just the way we like it." ❧

Linens and Lace (above and opposite) With views of the garden, these ocher-walled bedrooms are the place to be on Sunday mornings when the fog lifts and the room glows. Gary applied the carefully mixed and earth-tinted plaster in a gestural pattern. The project took him a week to complete as he waited for the plaster to dry in the rather damp climate. The beds are dressed with Italian heirloom linens.

POETICS OF PLACE

MARGARET GRADÉ *at Manka's Inverness Lodge in Inverness*

———

FOR MORE THAN A BAKER'S DOZEN YEARS, MANKA'S INVERNESS LODGE AND ITS SUPERB RESTAURANT HAVE BEEN AN INSIDER SECRET AMONG TOP CHEFS LIKE THOMAS KELLER, ORGANIC FOOD PURISTS LIKE THE PRINCE OF WALES AND THE Duchess of Cornwall (who have dined and slept there), as well as passionate urban aesthetes and food lovers. The lodge, a "private dining club" and a cluster of guest cottages in the redwoods, are situated near the Point Reyes National Seashore (established by John F. Kennedy) in Inverness, one of the smallest towns in California.

The object of their devotion is the creation of Margaret Gradé, a former neuropsychologist who acquired the rundown property in 1992. Built as a private hunting lodge in the twenties when the Point Reyes area was well stocked with deer and rabbits, the lodge had been purchased by a Czech family, who furnished it with plastic-veneered "suites" of furniture.

"I've spent a dozen years redesigning and remodeling it with handcrafted furniture in the Arts and Crafts–Adirondack manner so that it looks as if it hadn't been touched since the turn of the century," said Gradé,

who with her partner and co-chef, Daniel DeLong, has turned the restaurant into one of the finest and most original in the United States.

"My guiding intent is to elevate the daily events and requirements of living—eating and sleeping—to a level of celebration," said Gradé, who often starts the day by rowing across Tomales Bay to pick up fresh Hog Island oysters. "It is a particular joy of mine to play a part in the discovery of what it is to be sensually swept away by food that is raised, cooked, and presented with care."

Gradé learned to cook superbly by first studying the literature of food. "Far more moving to me than obsessing

---

Leaving the World Behind *(opposite)* Guests at Manka's Inverness Lodge slip easily into a dream state and time-travel to the twenties, thanks to Margaret's enhanced sense of theater and virtuoso style. Beside the log-burning fire (where she often grills quail or seasonal vegetables), she has created a witty corner suggesting fishing lodges, carefree days, and outdoor pursuits.

about it is to effectively rub together two sticks because one must stay warm, and then to create a blaze," she said. "I love the fact that Manka's appears so simple, so unassuming, as if just a joint off the road. If I had a choice, all our guests would come with the simple expectation of being fed, almost out of necessity. They would read the menu. All would sound familiar. And fine. And then, the carrot becomes more of a carrot than any they've had before—sublime! The duck egg more luxurious than they could have imagined. In this little idealized world of mine, that is, the kitchen, my goal is to make people feel excited simply by eating. I want them to feel satiated, and sexy."

Gradé seems to achieve her goals effortlessly.

"My goal is to create and maintain a place that bears testimony to personal integrity, and one which pays tribute to craftsmanship," she said.

There always seem to be carpenters, artists, stonemasons, gardeners, and painters working on projects, as guests blow in from a kayak trip or farmers and foragers, beekeepers, and wine makers deliver their finest meats, wine, figs, honey, fiddlehead ferns, wild mushrooms, fish, and splendid artisanal cheeses.

"It really is Daniel and I cooking in the kitchen,"

said Gradé. "We serve only locally produced ingredients. We don't think of ourselves as mavericks. I love to be told that the lives of our guests have been made richer, a bit fuller. But honestly, my greatest daily joy rests within contacts with our staff, and with growers, foragers, and fishermen, to whom I owe such credit."

Manka's is so low-key that often guests wander into the kitchen to chat with Gradé and DeLong.

"I love that time when I come into the lodge in the early-morning hours and no one in my midst is awake," she said. "My mission is to cook breakfast. I am surrounded by beauty. What luck. What more?

Sit Down Awhile (opposite) Fishing Cottage stands on the grounds of Manka's among the pine and redwood trees. A stone fireplace, a copper cauldron of firewood, and a large sofa invite guests to repose, read, gaze into the embers, and escape their everyday cares. A pair of sprung-leather club chairs await beneath the open window. Margaret Gradé's scene setting includes handwoven wool blankets, Pendleton blankets, an old bear rug, and a silver tray of local cheeses, quince paste, and fresh Fuji pears. Local organic wines are also offered.

Peace and Harmony (above) A king-size unpeeled-cypress bed covered in quilts, wool pillows, Pendleton blankets, and pure-white sheets makes a weekend visit memorable. Gradé has supplied collections of rare books, plus a secret window at each side of the bed. Guests vow never to leave.

"I also love closing time. I love to experience the restaurant staff—the 'people of the night,' as I call them—winding down, after being so 'on.' The show is over. The curtain closing is like the flag being lowered. It is like a wave good-bye in slow motion. Everything has been put back in place. Regardless of how ruddy the night may have been, it comes to a close in an elegant way. The slate is clean. It's always a clean close. That can't be said of many chapters in life."

Depending on the time of year, Gradé and DeLong may be found harvesting sea beans along the shore or visiting their honey supplier, or a cheese maker. To everything there is a season.

"I love the change of seasons," said Gradé. "Mine changes dramatically each month. Just as I'm tiring of one set of produce, one type of fish, one forager, we move into spring or summer. Early morning fog is replaced by an early burn-off. I love it when the restaurant staff arrive and bring the outside world with them. I can feel part of it for the moment. I love it when we are fluid enough with what we are cooking that day—which is different each day—to play music."

With beginner's mind, Gradé has created a lodge and restaurant, which seem to be a century old, with total integrity.

"When I bought the lodge I did not know the term *working capital*," she said. "In other words, I had none. And no experience which would have informed me that I should have some. Any extra money, of which there was pitiful little, was put back into the lodge. As a result, the advance was slow. I was forced to 'listen' to the lodge, and research revealed its history."

After a three-hour dinner, guests are inspired to wander into the garden for a walk in the moonlight or stargazing at Venus and Mars in the bright sky. Flashlight in hand, they return to Fishing Cottage. A fire is blazing in the stone hearth, and handmade caramels wait on the pillow. Ten leather-bound volumes of *The Library of the World's Best Literature* are stacked in an Adirondack cabinet beside the bed. A bottle of Robert Sinskey Vineyards organic Pinot Blanco stands on the oak table, with a basket full of walnuts and some chilled Fuji apples. You never want to leave. Welcome to the world of Manka's. ❧

Entered into with Abandon (opposite) Just one hour's drive from San Francisco, Manka's feels remote. This "little private dining club" serves organic cuisine soulfully crafted by Margaret Gradé and co-chef/co-owner Daniel DeLong. "Beef last seen grazing on H Ranch grasses" and "Tomales Bay mussels and Peter's Paradise Valley potatoes" were two recent menu items. To drink: 2002 Sean Thackrey Devil's Gulch Ranch Marin County Pinot Noir. On the sound system: Ivor Novello, Astor Piazzolla, Juliette Gréco, Anna Netrebko, Billy Eckstine.

PEACE AND PLENTY

The French Laundry, *a world-class restaurant in Yountville, Napa Valley*

———

CHEF THOMAS KELLER OPENED THE FRENCH LAUNDRY IN YOUNTVILLE ON JULY 6, 1994. EXTRAVAGANT PRAISE AND LOFTY AWARDS HAVE FOLLOWED HIS EVERY CHOP, SLICE, SIZZLE, STIR, AND DICE. KELLER'S SEDUCTIVE cuisine, with its exquisite white-on-white porcelain presentation, has won numerous awards for his utterly luxurious preparations of foie gras, Périgord truffles, and caviar, along with locally produced herbs, lemons, figs, and olive oils from his friends' gardens. In the kitchen, he marries the integrity and familiarity of classic preparation with the surprise, wit, and brevity of his modern interpretation.

In 1996 Keller was named the top chef in California by the prestigious James Beard Foundation, and in 1998 his restaurant was named the best in the United States by R. W. Apple in the *New York Times*. England's highly regarded *Restaurant* magazine voted The French Laundry the best restaurant in the world.

Lavish praise, indeed, for a small country restaurant in a quiet town in the Napa Valley. Thomas Keller's menus, fugues on unctuous bone marrow, golden duck eggs, fresh hearts of palm, and exquisite hand-harvested sea scallops, orchestrate impeccable seasonal ingredients and superb execution for the thinking gastronome, and lavish flavors and silken textures for the sensualist.

Keller's cuisine has turned fans into fanatics. Chef/best-selling food writer/television star Tony Bourdain calls Thomas Keller's cuisine "absolutely awe inspiring." As he recounts vividly in his TV program, *A Cook's Tour*, wild man Bourdain made his pilgrimage to the four-star French Laundry and went gunning for Keller. After twenty courses, he was charmed and seduced into a state of blissful submission—just like The French Laundry's passionate and happy guests, who often wait months for a choice table.

A Lesson in Harmony (opposite) The French Laundry restaurant, one of the most admired in the world, is approached across a flagstone terrace and beneath a rustic balcony. The structure, now updated, was originally built in 1890 on the corner of Washington Street and Creek Street in the center of Yountville, a small town in the heart of the Napa Valley. The name? It was a French steam laundry for several decades.

A Sense of Arrival (left and opposite) The French Laundry has just seventeen tables, and reservations are made two months in advance. Kathy Hoffman, the daughter of Sally and Don Schmitt, arranges seasonal flowers of breathtaking beauty. In fall, she choreographs pomegranate branches, lilies, berries, vines, and autumn leaves in subtle orange, gold, tawny, and harvest tones. In the low-key but elegant dining room, tables are set with pristine white linens, and perfectly pressed napkins are held in place with a wooden clothespin with The French Laundry logo.

The setting for this beauty and sensuality is a former French laundry, now gracefully transformed and restyled into a country restaurant of great charm. Iceberg roses bloom in the garden, and espaliered pears add a filigree of branches across a wall. Raked gravel, a stone wall, and a quirky stairway to a garden-viewing balcony are all carefully considered counterpoints to the ravishingly beautiful presentation of Keller's cuisine.

Ask Thomas Keller about what has propelled him to the top (his Per Se restaurant in New York brandishes three Michelin stars), and he responds that it's his elusive search for perfection, as well as a sense of work ethic, a desire to do a good job.

"I have an inner drive to achieve," he said. "I want to honor beautiful natural ingredients—and the people who produce them. I want to create sense memories for everyone who dines at The French Laundry. I love what I'm doing—every moment. It's essential to have a great team, and it helps to have a lot of stamina."

When asked how he creates rapture in the kitchen, his response is heartfelt, not intellectual.

"When I am cooking for friends and when I have an emotional connection with those who will be tasting, dining, that is a great feeling," he said. "Of course, I put everything into each dish I make, but for friends and family, it's especially meaningful."

Seasonal ingredients are always his jumping-off point.

"I am excited about what's beautiful in this world, and my obsession with ingredients consumes me every day," said the chef. "A perfect piece of striped bass, lamb, glass eels from Maine, God's creatures, white asparagus—I want to honor them, illuminate the flavors, make some kind of revelation about the tastes and colors. I'm also inspired by memories of food. The classic pickled eggs from the bar in my uncle's tavern are now translated into my eggs pickled in truffle juice in a Japanese porcelain bowl."

He dreams of a beautiful piece of poached Dover sole, fruit in season like summer figs or Meyer lemons, or blood oranges. They have their fleeting moments, and they are precious, he said. Keller pays homage to his favorite kitchen tools.

"I'm very fond of good, basic tools like a palette knife, which is perfect for lifting delicate objects and flexible enough to use for stirring and slicing," said the chef. "My newest favorite tool is an instant-read infrared oven thermometer. It's a precise instrument, and I appreciate precision. We can all be creative and spontaneous, but consistency, guaranteed by precise tools, is more important."

His goal is superb execution of everything—done with emotion and soul. "I want to be a great craftsman. It's a learned process of respect for ingredients."

His favorite compliment, he said, is "This reminds me of…" Success is creating memories— of a cherished moment, a person, a family tradition, and a special occasion.

A chef is only as good as his sources, Keller said.

"I have found the most amazing butter from Diane St. Clair, who owns Animal Farm in Orwell, Vermont. She makes it from organic Jersey milk three or four times a week, and it is incredibly rich and high in fat, yet delicate," said the chef.

On the market is his line of tableware for Raynaud—white Limoges porcelain, of course. He is working on a new inn with the New Mexico architect Antoine Predock, on three acres in Yountville. After the success of *The French Laundry Cookbook*, he produced *Bouchon*, a second hit.

Excellence, and passion, propel Keller through the maze of his ventures, which include a Las Vegas restaurant, best-selling books, an inn, and his kitchens. Perhaps the key to his success is that every project is very much in the spirit of The French Laundry, with an understated and classic aesthetic, and a precisely articulated point of view.

Fortunate guests who embark on a fifteen-course tasting menu, or a simple lunch know, too, that Keller and his team have perfected the art of seduction…one bite at a time. ❧

Fresh from the Garden (opposite) Chef/owner Thomas Keller insists on fresh seasonal ingredients in all dishes at The French Laundry. In a sunny plot across the road from the restaurant, culinary gardener Scott Boggs grows fresh French tarragon, beets, peas, chives, carrots, four varieties of spinach, French carrots, and waving branches of cardoons, a Keller favorite. Recent dishes on Tasting of Vegetables menus have included "Andante Dairy Acapella cheese with slow-baked baby beets, French Laundry garden Lollo Rossa lettuce, and Vidalia onion–mustard seed vinaigrette, K & J Orchard roasted chestnuts, celery branch batons, celeriac puree, shaved chestnuts, Tupelo honey–glazed cranberries, and cutting celery greens." Also on the menu: "Elysian Fields Farm selle d'agneau rôtie, wilted French Laundry garden Swiss chard leaves, glazed parsnips, golden Chanterelle mushrooms, and sauce aux pignons de pin," as well as "Fricassée of Musquée de Provence pumpkin, Brussels sprouts, Périgord truffle, and pomegranate seeds with beurre noisette." To accompany: Thomas Keller and Laura Cunningham's new Modicum wine.

THE FRENCH LAUNDRY

EARLY WONDER
BEET

ACKNOWLEDGMENTS

—

California Country Style has been the most rewarding, inspiring, and enjoyable project. Writing, selecting locations and residences, directing the photography, editing film, outlining layouts, and putting together this all-new book, I have crisscrossed the state, working with the most accomplished, passionate, and creative California people.

David Livingston's photography leaps off the pages. I have appreciated David's loyalty, flexibility, and steady hard work. It has been a great pleasure working with him.

I send special thanks to the leading interior designers, artists, antiques dealers, bibliophiles, philanthropists, teachers, professors, art collectors, photographers, architects, graphic designers, company presidents, floral designers, textile designers, innovators, inventors, gardeners, ranchers, farmers, winery owners, and furniture designers and their partners and friends, whose life work is depicted in this book.

I am delighted to showcase California's finest and most devoted creators, including my longtime friend Margaret Gradé, a world-class innkeeper and chef, and my old friend, chef Thomas Keller and his team: stars all the way. Warmest thanks to everyone on these pages who created the superb interiors, stylish retreats, modern weekend houses, classic decor, and even a clematis farm, a pear farm, and a walnut farm. Talent and devotion, indeed.

Heartfelt thanks to my superb editor, Lisa Campbell, who has been the most enthusiastic, charming, and joyful supporter of this wonderful book. I have appreciated Lisa's insight and team management, along with her great sense of elegance and style. Bouquets to Lisa!

San Francisco–based Madeleine Corson is an art director and graphic designer with a fantastic eye for proportion, type, and balance. I appreciate her professionalism, polished presentations, innate elegance, and focus.

Brooke Johnson at Chronicle Books is an outstanding art director, always encouraging and open to new ideas. Many thanks. Thanks also go to Mimi Kusch, our very organized copyeditor, and to production coordinator Beth Steiner.

My relationship with Nion McEvoy, the enlightened owner of Chronicle Books, and Jack Jensen, the energetic and insightful president of Chronicle Books, is one of long standing. Nion and Jack acquired my first book, *San Francisco: A Certain Style*, in 1988. All my subsequent books for Chronicle Books have stayed in print for many years and have been translated into Japanese and distributed throughout the world. I can walk into Galignani in Paris, Builder's Booksource in Berkeley, or Hatchard's in London and a design shop in Los Angeles, St. Helena, Sydney, New York, or Healdsburg, knowing I'll find my books there. I am delighted and grateful to continue to work with Nion and Jack and the talented staff of Chronicle Books. —D.D.S.

Wild in the Country (*opposite*) A tangle of fresh clematis at Chalk Hill Clematis expresses the chic and surprising new California country style.

INDEX